David Hendin was born in St. Louis, Missouri, and received B.S. and M.A. degrees from the University of Missouri. He is currently a member of the off-campus faculty of Missouri's School of Journalism.

Mr. Hendin is science editor of Newspaper Enterprise Association, the world's largest newspaper feature service. Since 1971 he has been a participant in the Task Force on Death and Dying of the Institute of Society, Ethics, and the Life Sciences. He is a member of the National Association of Science Writers and of the American Medical Writers Association. In 1972 Mr. Hendin was cited by the National Society for Medical Research "for science writing which has contributed significantly to public understanding of experimental medicine."

Mr. Hendin lives in Garnerville, New York, with his wife and daughter.

DEATH
AS A
FACT OF LIFE

DAVID HENDIN

WARNER
PAPERBACK
LIBRARY

A Warner Communications Company

WARNER PAPERBACK LIBRARY EDITION
First Printing: February, 1974

Library of Congress Catalog Card Number: 72-8883

This Warner Paperback Library Edition is published by arrangement
with W. W. Norton & Company, Inc.

Cover photograph by Al Freni

Warner Paperback Library is a division of Warner Books, Inc.,
75 Rockefeller Plaza, New York, N.Y. 10019.

Ⓦ A Warner Communications Company

To Lillian and Aaron Hendin, my parents,
I offer the ancient Hebrew toast,
L'chaim.

CONTENTS

INTRODUCTION

Why does a young writer devote a year of his life to an extensive look into a subject such as death? This is a question that, in one way or another, has been put to me dozens of times during the course of my work on this book. It is a question that, perhaps, could best be answered by my psychiatrist—if I had one. That viewpoint lacking, however, it seems to be left up to me alone to make this statement of personal intention.

When I first came upon the idea of writing a book on the realities of death and dying in our society, a number of my older friends and colleagues thought me presumptuous. "What," they asked, "could you possibly know about dying or death?" As a former biology teacher and professional medical and science journalist I felt that I knew, or could quickly grasp, more than most. Still, it was a question not to be ignored. After many hours of thought I realized that even at my relatively young age death had played an important role in my life. My mother died of leukemia before I was three. A favorite aunt died during my first year in college and I remember asking a close relative, before the funeral, what I should say to my cousin (the aunt's daughter). "I can't say that I'm sorry for her, for I feel just as sorry for myself."

The first time I pithed a frog in college zoology, destroying the animal's brain and in effect killing it, I wondered how that operation would have affected a man. The frog's heart and the rest of its body remained alive for days in the laboratory refrigerator, but for all intents and purposes it was dead with no brain function.

Five years later my grandfather lay in a nursing home progressively deteriorating from Parkinson's disease and atherosclerosis. I watched him change from the man who joyously took me on weekend outings to an individual who eventually did not recognize me, his own first grandson, and who lived in a world of delusion. I went home and cried for a day, for from that time on, although he lived for another year, he was dead in my mind. The grief that I suffered on learning of his death was not to be compared with that terrible day.

We all remember facing friends for the first time after one of their close relatives had died. What could we say? How could we relate to them? We said, "I know how you feel," but how could we? I was faced with such a situation on the day that I had to tell a college roommate that his father, a traveling salesman, had died in a motel room, in a strange city, of a heart attack. I watched his face as it changed from disbelief to anger, panic, and then calm maturity as he phoned his mother to tell her the news; and I watched his sorrow grow and then fade during the course of the next year.

We witness death on television and at the cinema, read daily news reports of how many were killed in war today. The Bomb could, and has, taken thousands of lives in an instant. This is the death we live with literally every day of our lives, but these deaths have become almost mechanical, we accept them as ordinary, to be expected and accepted. But accept our own deaths, never.

"We have shown an unmistakable tendency to put death aside, to eliminate it from life," wrote Sigmund Freud in 1918. Certainly death has become the taboo of our time. It is, in a very real sense, the last remaining one. Sex has been a taboo subject but it is no longer. Even elementary school students study it in their classrooms, all is open and above board. But who will talk to us about death, the inevitable end of life?

I have wondered what I would do if I learned I was dying, or my wife or parents or brothers. And as I researched this book I watched my wife's abdomen swell with new life, the life of my daughter who was conceived and born as this book was written.

Life and death. To exist and to exist no longer. I must believe that my thoughts and experiences are not unusual. Each of us must face them in his own time. But what do we learn, how do we prepare for the ending of life? Religious individuals can turn to their church, their clergymen, who may offer comfort, but may not. They may turn to their neighbor or physician, but these people, too, have been victims of the conspiracy of silence. We fear death but we do not discuss it. We expect it, but believe ourselves immortal.

"Go to any public library," wrote H. L. Mencken in *Smart Set* in 1919, "and look under 'Death: Human' in the card index, and you will be surprised to find how few books there are on the subject."

Even in 1972 Milton Mayer wrote of death in *If Men Were Angels,* "The paper-thin bibliography of the subject is eloquent testimony to the invincibility of our ignorance."

Actually, the bibliography is not that thin. There are books, monographs, and hundreds of papers; more are being published by the week. The trouble is that they are too often written by and for the specialist. Most persons have neither access to them nor the motivation to seek out these tomes written in the scientist's secret jargon.

It has only been in the past few years that physicians and even theologians have had courses on death and dying available in their professional training. Even today such courses are conspicuously absent at most of the nation's medical schools. Even if a medical school offers such a course this year, or next, how many years will it be before physicians with this type of information will be in the majority?

As a medical journalist I have been concerned over the problem of the length of time necessary to disseminate, in

11

a useful form, new information not only to the public, but to scientists.

It is hoped that this book will offer readers new information on death and dying in interesting and useful form. In addition to the act of dying I will deal with several moral, ethical, and scientific issues of our times. Each of them is "taboo" in the sense that people don't talk, won't talk, or haven't enough information to talk about them. When is a person dead? How does he go about donating his body or organs to science? Should he? What about euthanasia, the "good death," is it murder? Should we freeze people with an eye toward the time we may be able to bring them back to life? And what of the ecology of dying; the fact that the dead are already occupying too much valuable living space in cemeteries? And, of course, how can individuals better cope with death and grief for themselves and for their children?

Long and complicated discussions of the religious significance of death, and the afterlife, have not been included. These are questions each person must resolve for himself. Is there a soul, or isn't there? How many angels can dance on the head of a pin? Dozens of writers, each more astute than I, have discussed these questions. Their works are the classics of theology and philosophy.

This book is not meant to be all-encompassing, indeed it could not have been. Things are changing too fast.

Even with all of the information that is presented, it is possible that this book will not solve a single person's problems or dilemmas with regard to death and dying. But it may shock many, and anger some. If, however, it does nothing more than simply help to stimulate dialogue within every level of our society, then it will have served its purpose.

In a book such as this one, which contains hundreds of facts from many areas of biology, medicine, law, theology, and the social sciences, it would be impossible to name all the individual scientists and authors, journals and publications that have been consulted.

Most of the primary sources can be found in the bibliography, but I must offer a word of thanks to a few of the pioneers in the study of death and dying in our time: Dr.

Elisabeth Kübler-Ross, whose book, articles, and lectures are inspiring and invaluable; Dr. Austin Kutscher; Dr. Herman Feifel; Drs. Barney Glaser and Anselm Strauss, and Dr. Cicely Saunders.

Much information has been gleaned from interviews with individuals who have given unselfishly of their valuable time. Among them are Dr. Frank J. Ayd, Jr., Mrs. George Barclay, Mrs. Delia Batin, the Rev. Edward Dobihal, Rabbi Simon Greenberg, Frederick Horn, Dr. Julius Korein, Irving Ladimer, Mrs. Henri Mali, Dr. Desmond Morris, Dr. Bennett Olshaker, Judge Michael T. Sullivan, Mrs. Florence Wald, Dr. Alfred Weiner. In addition, numerous physicians and laymen have supplied anecdotes and case histories, and thus will remain anonymous.

In search of information I was also helped by many individuals and organizations, some of which I gratefully list here: The Rochester Institute of Technology; Babies Hospital, New York; The Columbia University College of Physicians and Surgeons; The Foundation of Thanatology; The Euthanasia Educational Fund; Gustavus Adolphus College; the *Honolulu Star-Bulletin;* United Press International; The American Academy of Family Physicians; Philip Merwin of New York University; The Cremation Association of America; the U.S. Department of Housing and Urban Development; H. Raymond Ligon; Finkelstein Memorial Library, Spring Valley, N.Y.; Roger Starr of the Citizen's Housing and Planning Council of New York; Dr. David Phillips, and my many journalist colleagues of the National Association of Science Writers who frequently helped me to gather clippings, seminar proceedings and other valuable material.

I am indebted to Dr. Leon Kass, chairman of the Task Force on Death and Dying of the Institute of Society, Ethics and the Life Sciences, and other task force members and Institute staff who graciously have allowed me to attend and participate in their most valuable discussions.

My thanks also go to Dr. Lawrence Lamb, Jack Kress, Dr. Irving Bengelsdorf, Robert Cochnar, and Hana Umlauf, all of whom were kind enough to read parts of the manuscript and make suggestions for improvement, as did my father, Dr. Aaron Hendin. Carol Houck Smith, of W. W. Norton & Company, Inc., reviewed the final draft of the manuscript and offered editorial criticism. The comments of all of the above individuals were carefully considered, and often implemented. The responsibility for any opinion or inaccuracy herein, however, must rest solely with the author.

A line, too, to thank my colleagues at Newspaper Enterprise Association, Inc., for their cooperation and tolerance, especially Robert Roy Metz, an understanding boss.

Finally, my heartfelt thanks to my wife, Sandra, for her help with all phases of the book from research to typing, from putting up with my work habits to suffering with me through the writing process. Her understanding helped the project through some difficult times.

DAVID HENDIN

June 1972

> "O death, where is thy sting?"
> *I Corinthians 15:55*

REVISING THE CRITERIA OF DEATH

Mrs. F., a plump woman of about fifty, sits in her gray, plastic-covered chair in a private room of a large Western hospital. It is the same chair she has been sitting in every day for the past seven weeks. Next to her, in the room's single bed, lies Ken, her oldest son.

"Ken," explains a physician familiar with the case, "is suffering from a rapidly fulminating type of multiple sclerosis." The twenty-two year old has been in a deep coma for nearly two months. He has not spoken or responded to any kind of attention. When open, his eyes hold only the most vacant stare. He cannot leave the bed and his body wastes are excreted, involuntarily, into plastic sacks connected to him by clear plastic tubes.

The boy's brain is gone, physicians say, and the rest of his nervous system is degenerating rapidly. He will never recover, never again will he be lucid. His heartbeat and breathing would have long ago stopped if artificial support measures had not been started and continued.

Ken's mother keeps close watch on the physicians handling the machines as well as the intravenous drips that supply her son with the only nourishment his body can handle.

"The boy," says the physician, "is a vegetable, he cannot recover. He will never recognize his mother, or anyone else again, yet she persists. Ken could be kept 'alive' like this for many more weeks. This doesn't make sense, he is a vegetable."

The hospital bill is more than $150 a day. Mrs. F. spends all her waking hours at the hospital—away from her home, her husband and two daughters.

"They are making themselves poor and she is letting this rip her family apart," the physician says.

Even if Mr. F. could bring himself to say something to his wife about the situation, it would do no good, the doctor adds. "The mother just cannot and will not accept the fact that her son is gone. 'There is still life, his heart is beating, he is breathing,' she maintains."

The heart *is* beating, he *is* breathing, but it is with mechanical support. Ken's brain is dead and cannot recover. Without the mechanical support his heart and lungs would have stopped working many days ago. Is this a living human being, or is it simply a biological preparation primed by machines?

"When do you pull the plug out and make this expensive equipment available to someone who might live?" asks Dr. Robert Schwab, a Harvard University neurologist.

For thousands of years the concept of the time of death was relatively simple and clearly defined. Death is—and always has been—the cessation of the functions of life. Today, however, the question of when death occurs has evolved into a more sophisticated problem: Which are the key functions of life? At what stage of arrest are they considered to mark the end of a human life? What is to be the role of artificial maintenance of some of these functions?

In recent years there has been a good deal of talk about a new definition for death. "You're not dead when your heart stops anymore. It's when your brain stops working," is a casual definition often tossed off in conversation nowadays. However, even according to the most recent medical knowledge this is simply not accurate. A person dies when his heart stops beating and his lungs stop functioning

16

irreversibly. It is *if,* and only if, these functions are being sustained by artificial means, as in the case of Ken F., that the physician may turn to newer criteria in determining death. This is necessary in a relatively few cases, but the number is increasing.

Early man associated life and living with breathing and, later, with circulation of the blood pumped by the heart (although the ancients did not tie the two together). As heartbeat and respiration waned and finally stopped it was only logical for our forebears to assume that life had left the body. In Genesis, according to some translations, it is written, "And Abraham expired, and died in a good old age." Thus, in biblical times death was recognized as the expiration of the mysteriously given spark of life. Little more was known.

As late as 1821, J. G. Smith's *Principles of Forensic Medicine* offered a rather confusing and relatively vague declaration of when death occurs. "If we are aware of what indicates life, which everyone may be supposed to know, though perhaps no one can say that he truly and clearly understands what constitutes it, we at once arrive at the discrimination of death. It is the cessation of the phenomena with which we are so especially familiar—the phenomena of life."

So, for a period covering most of written history, ending not too long ago, the end of life was determined by fairly straightforward criteria, even though those making the determinations were not quite sure about their basis in anatomical and physiological fact. It was simply known that when heartbeat and respiration stopped a man was dead. He did not come back. It soon became known, however, that this was not the whole story.

As man learned more of the wonderful complexities of the human body his curiosity about life and death broadened. In the eighteenth century new medical interest in death took a significant leap with the publication of a number of books and studies concentrating on the question of apparent death and "suspended animation." During this period organizations known as "humane" societies came into existence. It was the goal of these societies to save persons who had been drowned, asphyxiated, or struck by lightning, who were thus in a state confused with

17

death. The humane movement began in Europe, with the first society founded in Amsterdam in 1767. Others followed in Venice, Paris, London, Zurich, and other major cities of the day.

In 1780, the United States became involved in the movement with the formation of the Philadelphia Humane Society. A Massachusetts group was formed in 1786. (These humane societies which concerned themselves with humans are the forerunners of the animal humane societies that exist today. Some of today's humane societies, notably the American Humane Association headquartered in Denver, Colorado, still concern themselves with human, and the rest of the organization concentrates on animal AHA's efforts are directed toward child protective services and the rest of the organization concentrates on animal welfare.)

Even with their "humane" interests there was a great deal of controversy over the feasibility of the early humane movement's goals. A physician of the time, Benjamin Waterhouse, was invited to give the Massachusetts Society's annual lecture in 1790. He declared that "To blow in one's own breath into the lungs of another is an absurd and pernicious practice." But even in the face of such opposition and ridicule, William Hawes, of the Royal Humane Society in London, and others pressed ahead with the humane theory. With his own funds Hawes, an apothecary living near the river Thames, paid those who brought him drowned bodies within a short time after immersion. In 1780, in a broadly circulated "Address to the Public," he stated: "The AUTHOR likewise promises to pay the reward of ONE GUINEA to nurses or other attendants, *on any child or grown person returning to life* by their humane attention, provided the fact is ascertained by a *gentleman of the faculty,* or attested by three credible persons; and in hopes of exciting a universal attention to a subject of much importance to mankind."

Today the once controversial "humane" practice is called mouth-to-mouth, or artificial, respiration and is commonly practiced and taught to physicians and laymen alike. It has been responsible for saving many thousands of lives.

The gentlemen of the humane societies included some of the top medical men of the Enlightenment and they were notably successful in many areas of their work. A number of our present-day practices, such as death certificates signed by a physician, death houses, and prescribed delays of burials were initiated by the humane movement. The societies offered prizes and awards for essays on various aspects of resuscitation and death determination.

These physicians carefully examined all of the traditional signs of death accepted at the time, including cessation of pulse and breathing, pallor, coldness, relaxed sphincters, rigor mortis, and sometimes even the "only certain sign" of putrefaction. The movement was also responsible for the recognition of several new signs of death such as fixed, dilated pupils and auscultation of the heart. Subsequently, several additional "life tests" were developed. Notable among these was the blowing of a trumpet (seeking auditory response) and a test involving the application of electrical current to gain a muscular response from one thought to be dead.

Following the steps of the early humane movement, the medicolegalists of the 1800s often listed signs of death, but gave even more space to mistakes that might be made because of strict reliance upon those signs. For some the telling sign was rigor mortis, and others wrote at great length on the difference between that post-mortem stiffening of the body and tetanus, which has similar symptoms. Still others placed more reliance on newer criteria of the day such as the failure of muscles to contract upon application of electrical current.

Many of these early works were prompted by the fear, common in those days, of premature burial or autopsy and cases of suspended animation. Several ingenious gentlemen invented "indicators" to help determine whether a person had indeed been buried alive. The devices were often complicated gadgets to be placed in the grave. They would raise a flag or sound a warning in case the casket's occupant stirred. It was this macabre fear of being buried alive, as well as a fear of cruelty in burying other alive, that to a large extent prompted men to seek more information concerning the determination of death.

19

In 1890, the Prix Dusgate, a prize of twenty-five hundred francs, was awarded to a Dr. Maze who, in his belief that putrefaction was the only sure sign of death, advocated that cemeteries provide mortuaries where the bodies of deceased could lie until putrefaction began, thus eliminating all possibilities of mistaken burial. Still advocated as well were many tests to help eliminate the fear of premature burial. The tests, called for in many wills of the time, often consisted of having death proved surgically, by incision, or by application of boiling liquid or red-hot metal to the skin before burial was attempted.

Today, after centuries of medical progress, after the passing of the humane movement, our description of the visible signs of death remains the same. In his popular book *The Old Person in Your Home,* Dr. William Poe offers the following description: "The eyes become fixed, with opened pupils which do not respond to light. The heartbeat and breathing cease. The mouth may be open and motionless. The skin turns pale and cold. The skin in contact with the bed may become bluish or purple—livor mortis. After thirty to sixty minutes the limp extremities may become stiff—rigor mortis."

To the casual observer these have always been the visible manifestations of death. But today there is a necessity to describe the phenomenon on other levels. Death is variously determined by different academic disciplines: Medical death refers to the cessation of the functions of human life; biological death refers to the cessation of the simple life processes of the various organs and tissues of the body; theological death is generally held to designate the moment at which the soul leaves the body; and legal death occurs when the courts say it has.

If modern technologies had not muddied the issue, Dr. Poe's definition, or even much earlier ones, would suffice for the sophisticated physicians of today. No matter how much discussion there has been or will be to confuse the facts, under normal circumstances, when respiratory and circulatory functions irreversibly cease, a man is dead. These criteria have always sufficed, because without these two vital functions, blood would not circulate in the body and the brain would not be supplied with the precious oxygen it needs to stay alive.

Now, in an ever-increasing number of cases, technological interventions have made these signs insufficient as criteria for determining death. Everyday in hospitals around the world hearts are restarted by cardiac massage, chemical agents, electric shock, and artificial respiration. We have respirators, pacemakers, heart-lung machines, and even the possibility of completely artificial hearts. The use of such devices can, in some cases, indefinitely preserve breathing and heartbeat. The dream of the humane societies has come to pass.

It is no longer unusual for a patient to be revived from death (or what certainly would have become death a few years ago) by heart attack, accidents, drowning, extreme cold, or electrocution. And if humane society member William Hawes today offered one guinea for each person so revived, he would run out of money in a very short time. Large numbers of "deaths" occur from heart stoppage in the course of or immediately after surgery, so most hospitals maintain emergency warning systems which are attached to the patient. Twenty-four-hour-duty crews of specialists and resuscitation equipment stand ready to move into action as soon as an alarm signaling a cardiac arrest sounds. One patient who died by the old "heart-stoppage definition" more than ninety times, was five years later carrying on an active schedule wearing a cardiac pacemaker assuring satisfactory heart function.

"I remember when cessation of heartbeat was an observation on which we simply pronounced the patient dead; now, this is a medical syndrome known as cardiac arrest," says Dr. William P. Williamson of the University of Kansas in the *Journal of the American Medical Association*. "Cessation of respiration is a symptom also formerly implying death, which can now be corrected by an ingenious and devilishly efficient machine known as a mechanical respirator."

Today, when the criteria for death take on significance undreamed of by physicians in earlier times, our modern medical techniques have made arriving at such criteria more difficult. Arising from the possible confusion and uncertainty are situations which may bring about far-reaching consequences to many elements integral to the framework of society. Matters relating to homicide, burial, transplantation, family relations, voting by proxy, and wills are linked to a clear and concise notion of whether a person is dead or alive. Moreover, severe social, economic, and psychological problems can arise among the loving next of kin because of life-or-death ambiguities.

Must physicians today continue to rely on breathing and heartbeat as the critical death signs? In cases where mechanical intervention has played an important role surely it would be wiser to consider the condition of the brain as critical. It is no coincidence that for the thousands of years that the heart was thought to be the seat of man's emotion, heart death was considered life's final insult. Although we still speak of the heart's role idiomatically—"have a heart"—we know now that it is the brain that controls man's intellect and emotions. Thus it is only natural that modern man turn, if necessary, to brain death as the critical sign of death.

Hannibal Hamlin, a Boston neurosurgeon, has noted that "although the heart has been enthroned through the ages as the sacred chalice of life's blood, the human spirit is the product of man's brain, not his heart." Dr. Denton Cooley expressed a similar opinion. "The brain is the only privileged organ in the body. The personality, mind, spirit, soul, and other intangibles must reside in the brain . . . it allows for cognition, integration of information, and concentrated thought . . . which distinguishes man from all other species."

It is also true, of course, that until relatively recently there was no quantitative way to measure brain activity. After all, even the earliest physicians recognized the heart's incessant throbbing as a sign of life. For a medical man to determine whether a person's heart was still beating it was only necessary to put his ear to the other's chest. Various instruments such as the stethoscope, or better yet the electrocardiograph, improved on this; but for the most part it has been a relatively simple matter to determine whether a heart was beating.

Today with our increased knowledge of human anatomy and function, and the introduction of the electroencephalograph (EEG), a machine that measures the electrical activity in the cortex of the brain, we have also begun to learn how to determine brain death.

Although it was the improvement in resuscitative and supportive techniques that led physicians to the realization that new criteria for defining death were needed, it was the surgical revolution—peaking with the first heart transplants of the late 1960s—that did more than any other event or series of events in history to blur the shadowy line between the quick and the dead. Vital organ transplantation demanded revised criteria for death.

Indeed the lack of such universally acceptable criteria kept at least one eminent physician from greater fame and fortune and, perhaps, cost the life of at least one of his patients. Dr. James D. Hardy, a surgeon at the University of Mississippi, was the first to perform a human lung transplant. Except for a series of unusual circumstances, he might have been the first physician to perform a human-to-human heart transplant—years before Dr. Christiaan Barnard's first successful human heart transplant at Groote Schuur Hospital in South Africa in 1967. Several times Dr. Hardy had potential donors ready, keeping them alive by mechanical means. But the time was never quite opportune for the potential recipients. On one occasion, in 1964, the recipient was ready and the surgeons did not feel he could survive without a heart transplant. But they could not, with certainty, pronounce the potential donor dead, so they transplanted into the recipient's chest a heart taken from a chimpanzee. The simian heart continued to beat for about ninety minutes, but it proved inadequate to keep the patient's body supplied with life-giving blood and the recipient died. Who can say what the result might have been if the surgeons could have definitely pronounced the donor dead and proceeded with the human-to-human heart transplant?

Other curious problems have arisen because of the lack of a firm definition of death. After a heart transplant in 1968 by Texas surgeon Denton Cooley, lawyers became interested in a subtle legal problem. The donor of the heart, Clarence Nicks, had been badly beaten and had suffered brain injury in a barroom brawl. At Houston's St. Luke's Hospital his brain registered no electrical activity and he had no reflexes for hours. He would never have regained consciousness, so the machine which was providing oxygen to his blood was turned off and his heart was transplanted to John Stuchwish, who lived for a number of days. There was concern among physicians and lawyers over whether the trial of Nick's assailant might be hampered by surgical removal of the victim's heart, thus preventing the legally valid autopsy necessary in homicide cases. The Cooley team proceeded only after a county medical officer agreed not to take action against them for "hiding" or "destroying" evidence—in this case a living human heart. (One is reminded of Edgar Allan Poe and the "Telltale Heart"!) Furthermore, lawyers for the man charged with killing Nicks could conceivably have argued that the victim died, not when his brain ceased to function and he was officially pronounced dead, but later that day when surgeons removed his heart which, while not actually beating, was "faintly quivering" according to Dr. Cooley. Was Clarence Nicks killed in the fight or murdered by the physician who removed his heart? Or more confounding still, was Nicks alive since his heart was beating inside Stuchwish? Was Stuchwish, whose heart had been removed and disposed of, really dead? If you were a member of a jury deliberating this case, what would your verdict be?

In such a case the major question to be considered is, "When is the moment of death?"

It must be recognized, however, that there can be no such thing as an exact moment of death, except in the exacting and rarefied atmosphere of the courtroom. "Isn't it true, doctor, that the victim died at exactly 9:52 A.M.," Perry Mason might have asked, for such specifics are often demanded by the law. But it is recognized that death takes place as a sequence of events. "Death is a process and not a moment in time, as the law believes," says Dr. Pierre H. Muller of France in the *World Medical Journal.* "During the process there are a series of physical and chemical changes, starting before the medico-legal time of death and continuing afterward." In the sequence of death there is a point of irreversibility that can generally be diagnosed by physicians. When this point is reached, nothing more can be done to restore intelligent life.

In line with beliefs concerning a sequence of death, is the interesting statement made by a physician in 1836:

"Individuals who are apparently destroyed in a sudden manner, by certain wounds, diseases or even decapitation, are not really dead, but are only in conditions incompatible with the persistence of life." This was an early distinction between somatic death, the extinction of personality, and cellular death.

The death of a man, the ebbing away of life from one stage of viability to another, may be slow or quick. The speed of the process depends on age, physical constitution, the patient's environment, and the cause of dying. Whatever the circumstances surrounding life's decline, however, in most cases there is an orderly progression from clinical death, to brain death, to biological death, and finally cellular death.

Clinical death occurs when spontaneous respiration and heartbeat irreversibly cease. The blood stops circulating and the brain is deprived of oxygen. Unless artificial resuscitation is started immediately brain death follows clinical death quickly since the brain, at normal body temperature, cannot survive oxygen starvation for more than a few moments. Nor are brain tissues capable of healing or regenerating as are most other tissues in the body. If resuscitative measures are begun at the moment of clinical death—depending on death's cause—life may be restored and it is possible for the patient to fully recover. On the other hand, brain death may still occur shortly or eventually in spite of resuscitation efforts.

Just as the body dies in steps, so too does the brain. In oxygen starvation, called anoxia, the first part of the brain to die is the highly evolved cerebral cortex, the section of the brain where sensations are registered and voluntary actions are initiated. The cerebral cortex is the part of the brain which participates in memory storage, where decisions are made and higher thought processes occur.

The midbrain is next, and then the brain stem dies. If there is irreversible destruction of the higher levels of the brain, the cerebrum, without damage to the brain stem—the primitive, vital center in the lower levels of the nervous system—there is a permanent loss of consciousness, but heart and breathing functions can go on. Even if the more primitive parts of the brain—those that evolved early in

25

man's history—are irreversibly damaged it still may be possible to maintain body functions for some time.

When all of the components of the brain are dead, biological death, or the permanent extinction of bodily life, occurs. Within a short time cellular death begins; because of differences in cellular composition, different parts of the body die at different times. This is the reason that a viable organ can be removed, preserved for a short time, and successfully transplanted after biological death has occurred. For this reason, too, even after biological death, organs within the lifeless body can be kept alive for a time by mechanical and/or chemical means. (As many physicians have pointed out, if a guillotine has cut off a person's head, it is possible today to keep his heart and lungs going for days.)

Similarly, while brain death rapidly follows the cessation of blood circulation, many cells of the body continue to live for some time after the body's death. Muscles, for example, will respond to electrical stimuli for up to two hours. Hair and nails may continue growing for a day or longer. Groups of cells can even be removed from the body after death and kept alive and functioning, sometimes indefinitely, in an artificial tissue culture.

Nevertheless, the idea of removing a *living* organ from a *dead* person remains a matter of controversy to many. Discussion of who draws the line and when has led to some grim speculations. On a visit to the United States shortly after his first transplant operation in December 1967, Dr. Christiaan Barnard was interviewed by a Soviet news correspondent in New York. The reporter cabled the following dispatch to his paper, *Komsomolskaya Pravda:* "Just imagine a bandit corporation which deals with the murder of people only for the sake of selling their organs on the black market. These goods would be needed by doctors for their rich clients. Money could make doctors register death before it happened."

Apparently such a situation could never arise in the Soviet Union. Dr. Joseph J. Timmes, professor of surgery at the New Jersey College of Medicine and Dentistry, at the 1968 symposium "The Moment of Death," explained: "I spoke with surgeons in the Soviet Union while visiting the medical institutes in Leningrad and in Moscow. To the question of how they defined the moment of death, they answered that this was not a serious problem in the Soviet Union, the reason being that all bodies belong to the State. When an individual dies—meaning when he is pronounced dead—physicians can perform an autopsy or remove an organ without consent of the next of kin, as is legally required in this country."

After a few of the early heart transplants in the United States, Dr. Carl Wasmuth, then president of the American College of Legal Medicine, explained that death comes when the physician "has done everything to save the patient's life and comes to the point where he feels the patient can't live. Once a man makes up his mind to stop that respirator or cardiac pacemaker, from that minute the patient is dead."

A federal public health official in Washington voiced his fears late in 1967 when he said, "I have a horrible vision of ghouls hovering over an accident victim with long knives unsheathed, waiting to take out his organs as soon as he is pronounced dead."

Farfetched? Perhaps. But there have been a number of publicized cases involving the unresolved issue of when a person dies. One took place in Stockholm in 1966, when surgeon Clarence C. Crafoord of the famed Karolinska Institute (which annually awards Nobel Prizes) removed a kidney from a dying woman with irreversible and irreparable brain damage. He transplanted it to a patient with kidney disease. The husband of the deceased had consented, but a furor was raised both inside and outside the medical profession.

"Don't keep already dead people alive," Dr. Crafoord countered. "A surgeon must feel that it is not his duty to give help to a person whose brain does not function. . . . What I want is a modern moral, ethical, religious, medical, and legal definition of the death concept. The basis for such a definition must be: you are dead when your brain doesn't function any more—not when your heart has stopped beating. When the electrical activity of one's brain stops—which can be measured—life is gone and what's left is only a surviving organism which can be used to save the lives of other people."

In making the suggestion that a person should be declared dead when a flat EEG pattern showed his brain had irrevocably ceased to function, Dr. Crafoord was concerned with truly hopeless cases. But the relatives of patients being kept alive by mechanical devices jumped to the conclusion that he meant the devices should be shut off, the patients declared dead, and their organs used for transplants.

France's National Academy of Medicine soon added to the furor with their recommendation that a patient may be considered dead if the EEG showed no brain activity for forty-eight hours. After that amount of time, the Academy recommended, the patient could be declared officially dead by a committee of three physicians, even if he was being kept alive artificially. Thus physicians could use mechanical means to keep the potential donor's organs viable —even though he was officially dead—until they were needed for transplantation.

Also in 1966, at Massachusetts General Hospital, Harvard neurologist Robert Schwab said that for a patient to be considered dead, the EEG must remain flat for about twenty-four hours, and stay flat in spite of external stimuli such as loud noises. The patient must have no heartbeat *or* respiration of his own, and no reflexes of the muscles or eyes. "After that," said Dr. Schwab, "the physician in charge can agree to turn off the artificial aids and pronounce the patient dead."

Most scientists argue that the specific amount of time the EEG must remain flat depends on the circumstances surrounding the patient's condition. Since there is no regeneration of brain tissue, scientists know that if certain brain cells are deprived of oxygen for more than a few seconds they will die, never again to recover their function. But the more primitive parts of the brain, those that control the vital functions, can live for longer times. So it is possible for the individual to lose personality, thought, and voluntary movement, and still survive as a vegetable because the vital centers of the brain are intact. Thus one could consider that after five minutes of a flat EEG reading, meaningful life is extinct. Some biologists accept a shorter time—as short as one minute—as proof of death, while others adhere to the twenty-four- or forty-eight-hour time limits.

Nevertheless, there are striking exceptions. One of these is severe barbituarate poisoning, as often is the case in attempted suicide. Another exception is when a person has undergone a long exposure to extremely low temperatures such as those reached by the hypothermic—body cooling to temperatures below 90 degrees Fahrenheit—techniques used in some modern heart surgery. The patients in such cases may have flat EEG readings for several hours and still be capable of complete recovery. Under these circumstances, although the patient appears dead by conventional standards, he is actually in a temporary state of artificially induced hibernation or suspended animation. In some cases where barbiturate poisoning or low temperatures are not factors, however, the question is how much of the brain has already been destroyed? At what point should the physician be permitted, or obligated, to pull the plug?

"When the circumstances justify it," says Dr. Frank J. Ayd, Jr., editor of the *Medical-Moral Newsletter,* "the law should recognize that a person should be permitted to discontinue extraordinary means of sustaining life when clinical death is imminent and inevitable. Instead doctors should be required to alleviate suffering only and not make extraordinary efforts to prolong life."

In 1957, at the International Congress of Anesthesiologists in Rome, Pope Pius XII was asked, "When does a death occur?"

His answer was, "Human life continues for as long as its vital functions, distinguished from the simple biological life of the organ, manifest themselves spontaneously without the help of artificial processes. . . . The task of determining the exact instant of death is that of the physician."

Dr. Joseph Fletcher, formerly of the Episcopal Theological School in Cambridge, Massachusetts, explains that when "positively" inevitable the speeding up of a donor's death may be justified if a subsequent transplant will provide another human being with valuable life. But Chief Rabbi Immanuel Jakobovits of Great Britain disagrees:

29

"Even a fraction of life is precious. Therefore, no one must hasten the death of a donor," he explains, following age-old Talmudic philosophy. Other more liberal rabbis might more readily agree with Dr. Fletcher.

Indeed, the decision of when the human spirit is gone, when to turn off the machines, is a moral as well as a medical and legal problem. The physician, trained from his first day in medical school that his duty is to save and prolong life, may resort not only to extraordinary measures, but he may persist well after there is any real hope of recovery. The problem of determination of death is one with which the physicians simply must live—even if there are some who deny that the subject is even open to debate.

At a meeting in July 1968, in Capetown, South Africa, for example, there was little controversy among thirteen heart transplant surgeons over the question of determination of death. The reason was "probably because all of us had answered this question for ourselves a long time ago," Dr. Denton Cooley explained. During the meeting the surgeons did agree that neurological examination and EEG tracings should show no signs of cerebral activity if death was to be declared. But, "we did not define the length of time this should be so," Dr. Cooley said. "In most heart transplants performed to date, this period exceeded two hours. In two of my donors there was a flattened EEG for four days prior to transplant."

In June, the month before the Capetown meeting, the Council of the Organizations of Medical Science met in Geneva and set forth their criteria for determination of death. In essence they said that cerebral function must have completely and irreversibly ceased, but they set no time limits. The criteria for cessation of cerebral function set forth in Geneva are as follows:

1. Loss of all response to the environment
2. Complete loss of reflexes and muscle tone
3. Absence of spontaneous respiration
4. Massive drop in arterial blood pressure when not artificially maintained
5. An absolutely linear electroencephalographic tracing recorded under the best technical conditions, even with artificial stimulation of the brain

Two months later the World Medical Assembly met in Sydney, Australia. Their statement on death, referred to as the Declaration of Sydney, seemed to side-step the problem of precisely defining death:

The determination of the time of death in most countries is the legal responsibility of the physician and should remain so. . . . A complication is that death is a gradual process at the cellular level, with tissues varying in their ability to withstand deprivation of oxygen. But clinical interest lies not in the state of preservation of isolated cells, but in the fate of a person. Here the point of death of the different cells and organs is not so important as the certainty that the process has become irreversible by whatever techniques of resuscitation that may be employed.

This determination will be based on clinical judgment supplemented if necessary by a number of diagnostic aids, of which the electroencephalograph is currently the most helpful. However, no single technological criterion is entirely satisfactory in the present state of medicine, nor can any one technologic procedure be substituted for the overall judgment of the physician. If transplantation of an organ is involved, the decision that death exists should be made by two or more physicians, and the physicians determining the moment of the death should in no way be immediatedly concerned with the performance of the transplantation.

The group's president, Sir Leonard Mallen, commented on the WMA declaration: "With scientific advances and new methods of resuscitation always coming up, it would be silly of us to give a definition which could be outmoded within half an hour."

Reflecting the growing concern over the lack of accepted guidelines for new criteria for death, in the same month the WMA met, August 1968, a committee of Harvard University scholars—physicians, theologians, lawyers, and philosophers—proposed their own set of guidelines. The Ad Hoc Committee's yardstick was one that others had already used, or hinted at: brain death—clearly irreversible coma.

Published in the *Journal of the American Medical As-*

31

sociation, the panel's recommendations were that a patient be judged dead on four grounds.

1. *Unreceptivity and Unresponsivity.* There is a total unawareness to externally applied stimuli and inner need and complete unresponsiveness—our definition of irreversible coma. Even the most intensely painful stimuli evoke no vocal or other response, not even a groan, withdrawal of a limb, or quickening of respiration.

2. *No Movements or Breathing.* Observation covering a period of at least one hour by physicians is adequate to satisfy the criteria of no spontaneous muscular movements or spontaneous respiration or response to stimuli such as pain, touch, sound or light. . . .

3. *No Reflexes.* Irreversible coma with abolition of central nervous system activity is evidenced in part by the absence of elicitable reflexes. The pupil will be fixed and dilated and will not respond to a direct source of bright light. . . .

4. *Flat Electroencephalogram.* Of great confirmatory value is the flat or isoelectric EEG. We must assume that the electrodes have been properly applied, that the apparatus is functioning normally, and that the personnel in charge is competent. . . .

These requirements, according to the panel headed by Dr. Henry K. Beecher, must be met for at least a twenty-four-hour period. If the patient shows no improvement, he can safely be considered dead. It is extremely important to note, however, that specifically excluded from these requirements are individuals under the effect of hypothermia or suffering from overdoses of central nervous system depressants such as barbiturates.

To emphasize the validity of their criteria, the Harvard group cited one study in which the post-mortem state of the brain was coordinated with the predeath findings such as those describing irreversible coma. The brain was obviously destroyed in 128 patients examined, and in the study, "not one gave any evidence of viable brain tissue."

In another study only three of more than twenty-five hundred patients with flat EEGs for up to twenty-four hours recovered. The three who survived were under the effects of central nervous system depressants and therefore outside the limits set by the panel.

The Harvard committee further recommended that when the brain is demonstrably dead, two physicians—one a neurologist or neurosurgeon—may agree to inform the family that the respirator is to be turned off. "It is pointless and needlessly cruel to ask the family to make this decision," they said. Only after this action has been taken should a transplant team enter the situation. Then artificial respiration can be continued almost indefinitely, preserving most of the organs for furture use.

Neither the Harvard proposals, nor any of the other sets of suggested guidelines—no matter how much prestige they represent or how specific they are—carry any official or legal weight, except to the extent that in the United States, in any legal case, it is the medical consensus that determines what death is. Thus general acceptance by physicians of a given set of criteria could lead to a revised legal conception of death merely by widespread use and acceptance.

The Harvard guidelines have probably been those most readily accepted so far. As one member of the Harvard group noted recently, "Since the publication of the report, the clinical recommendations have been accepted and followed on a world-wide basis in a most gratifying fashion."

Reports such as those emanating from the Harvard committee are prepared in behind-closed-door sessions where doctors, lawyers, and theologians express their diverging views. The discussions are likely to be rarefied, and not always related to the actual everyday needs of practicing physicians. Some concerned physicians have indeed complained about this, for it is not in the halls of academia, but in hospitals and courtrooms where guidelines must stand the test. If reports and guidelines can lead to action, then an evolution in current practice begins to take place.

Such an evolution regarding criteria for death is undoubtedly taking place. It should be stressed, though, that this is evolution, not revolution. None of the proposals for new criteria are meant to replace the traditional criteria for determining death. Scientists make it clear that they should complement them. We should avoid "the notion that the new criteria constitute a new *definition* of death, rather than a refined and alternative means for detecting the same 'old' phenomenon of death," says the prestigious Task Force on Death and Dying of the Institute of Society, Ethics and the Life Sciences.

Many physicians understand this, but others still may not. And the majority of laymen are left in a state of confusion. The blame for such confusion must fall upon physicians and scientists, who are often overprotective and secretive wth their pronouncements, as well as upon the various mass media which may not have discussed this very important subject thoroughly or accurately.

Some professionals have criticized any direct public involvement in the process of medical change. But it is the superficial presentation of new medical knowledge that has caused the public's apprehension, and public education is needed to set the record straight. If physicians alone are to be empowered with changing the rules by which life itself is measured, the public wants protection from the possibility that heartless or greedy physicians may follow their own selfish interests. Likewise, the majority of physicians wish to seek protection for themselves against expensive, time-consuming, and often professionally damaging malpractice suits that could easily arise over questions concerning determination of death.

These considerations have led to suggestions for legislative action. Interestingly, however, the overwhelming body of opinion in the legal and medical professions has been opposed, holding that the criteria describing death are matters to be determined by physicians, not legislators.

Referring to the prospect of legislative action in this regard, Dr. Irving Wright, emeritus professor of clinical medicine at Cornell University Medical College, said at a 1968 symposium, "Heaven forbid! While wise men of all disciplines may well voice their views, and even suggest guidelines of action, at this early stage in the new era it would be the height of folly to develop new rigid rules which might have legal status."

Such sentiment is backed up by the fact that, currently in most of the United States, the question of human death

34

is looked upon as a question of fact to be decided in each case. Courts seek expert medical testimony when doubt exists. The current status of the law is that a person is dead when a physician, basing his decision on ordinary standards of medical practice, says he is.

In the belief that this case-law background was not sufficient to deal with current situations, the state of Kansas, in 1970, took the first statutory step in the common-law world and enacted into law "definitions" of death. The Kansas statute establishes two alternative "definitions of death." These are permanent absence of spontaneous respiratory and cardiac function, and permanent absence of spontaneous brain activity. The specific criteria are left to "ordinary standards of medical practice."

Both the desirability and the wording of the Kansas statute have been highly controversial. It is clear to all involved that the laws in this area must change, but these changes need not necessarily come only through legislation.

"No statutory change in the law should be necessary since the law treats this question as one of fact to be determined by physicians," the Harvard Committee stresses. The group adds that such legislation would only be necessary in the case of great controversy.

There does not seem to be any great controversy within the medical profession. Still, a number of other states have begun to consider legislation similar to the Kansas statute. Early in 1972, Maryland became the second state to enact such a law.

Dr. William Curran, professor of legal medicine at Harvard, argues that such statutes "are absolutely necessary to protect doctors and enable them to save lives." The Kansas and Maryland statutes, he notes, have been "opposed by some lawyers who feel the courts should continue to follow the common law and go by new case law as cases come up. I don't think that makes sense at all. It's like letting speed laws be established by lawsuits resulting from crashes."

Still, thoughtful individuals ask, "Why the rush?" to formulate statutory law, for this type of law can be confusing, imprecisely drafted, or overly rigid. Movements by some states in the Kansas direction, however, have encouraged even those opposed to such legislation to begin the process of drafting ideal statutes to be used as prototypes. "If we are going to have a law, it might as well be a useful one," commented one scientist who did not favor legislation but found himself caught between the possibility of a sensible statute or a stifling one. The scientist, who asked not to be identified because of the circumstances surrounding his statements, is of the belief that the current laws and regulations covering determinations of death are sufficiently flexible.

Black's Law Dictionary (1951), a standard legal reference, defines death as "The cessation of life; the ceasing to exist; defined by physicians as a total stoppage of the circulation of the blood, and a cessation of the animal and vital functions consequent thereupon, such as respiration, pulsation, etc."

In one case, the Arkansas Supreme Court ruled that the *Black's* definition was not even open to further argument. In 1958, in the case of *Smith v. Smith,* Hugh Smith and his wife Lucy Coleman Smith were involved in an automobile accident. At the scene of the accident Hugh Smith was found dead. His wife was unconscious and taken to the hospital. In each of their wills they had named the other as executor and neither provided an alternate executor. The couple had no children.

Ostensibly it was clear that Mrs. Smith was the survivor, since on probate of the estate it was noted that she "remained in coma due to brain injury" and died at the hospital seventeen days later. Under these circumstances Mrs. Smith had inherited all of her husband's estate. When she died the estate then passed on to her descendants.

If, however, both had been killed simultaneously, the dispersal of the estate would have been left to the court and the possibility existed that Hugh Smith's heirs would have been involved in the estate.

With that reasoning, a nephew of Hugh Smith's petitioned the court and argued that both Hugh and Lucy Smith, "deceased, lost their power to will at the same instant and that their demise as earthly human beings occurred at the same time in said automobile accident, neither of them ever regaining any consciousness whatsoever."

The petition was dismissed as a matter of law. The court quoted from *Black's* definition and said, "Admittedly, this condition did not exist, and as a matter of fact, it would be too much of a strain of credulity for us to believe any evidence offered to the effect that Mrs. Smith was dead, scientifically or otherwise, unless the conditions set out in the definitions existed."

The court also added that "We will take judicial notice that one breathing, though unconscious, is not dead."

"Judicial notice," in this instance, means that the court did not consider *Black's* definition open to controversy. The question was considered as already settled in responsible medical and scientific circles. In making such a statement, the judge made proof of uncontroverted facts unnecessary. This prevented a drawing out of the trial and avoided the possibility of a perpetration of fraud on the court by unethical "scientists for hire" who might, for a price, come into court and raise questions about settled scientific principles.

The most bizarre extension of this absolute definition of death was made in a Kentucky court of appeals in the case of *Gray v. Sawyer*. In this case Mr. and Mrs. Leonard Gugel were killed by a locomotive at a railroad crossing. Since the court had no way of determining who had died first it was adjudged that they died simultaneously. Later, however, suit for a new trial was filed on the ground of newly discovered evidence.

The new evidence was provided by a woman who lived near the scene of the accident. At the time of the accident she had heard the noise and went to see what had happened. She found Mrs. Gugel decapitated, her head lying about ten feet from her body, which was actively bleeding "from near her neck and blood was gushing from her body in spurts."

At stake was the right to administer the will, but the decisive point was survivorship of one of the dead. The court stated:

37

Realistically, a person is dead when there has been a complete decapitation of the head, as was proved in the original case; but upon a hypothetical question submitting the above statements of [the new witness] and, as well, the terrific mangling of the body of her husband and other conditions relating to both, several doctors expressed the opinion that Mrs. Gugel had survived her husband for a fleeting moment. The doctors told the court that a body is not dead so long as there is a heart beat and that may be evidenced by the gushing of blood in spurts. This is so though the brain may have quit functioning.

Thus it would seem that the court had ruled that the woman did survive her husband and that the petitioner, Mrs. Gugel's father, Thomas Gray, would have the right to administer the estate. The court, however, ruled against Gray on a procedural technicality.

In both *Smith v. Smith* and *Gray v. Sawyer,* the courts held exclusively to the heart stoppage definition of death. But in May of 1972, for the first time in any court, a judge allowed his jury to consider the concept of brain death as well as heart death in making a decision. The precedent-setting case had begun almost exactly four years before, in May 1968, when physicians at the Medical College of Virginia decided to use for the world's seventeenth human heart transplant the heart of Bruce O. Tucker, a fifty-four-year-old black laborer who had suffered massive brain damage in an accident. Tucker's brother William contended that the donor was alive when his heart was removed, that the physicians, in effect, had killed him. His evidence was that machines were maintaining the man's vital life signs—circulation and breathing. Medical witnesses, however, held that Tucker had been dead for several hours according to the brain-death definition. The seven-man jury agreed that a man whose brain is dead is truly dead.

The only reason the jury could have made such a decision was that Judge A. Christian Compton told the jury it could heed either the classic definition of death or the newly revised one. The jury also was charged with deciding whether the classic signs of life were being maintained by machines or nature. By accepting the argument of the defense the jury agreed—as the Kansas and Maryland statutes covering death stipulate—that death is basically a medical concept, not a legal one. They recognized that physicians' methods of determining death may be refined from year to year. The fact is that the specifics of determining death may even vary from one physician to the next.

"Diagnosis is always statistical, never absolute," declares Bellevue Hospital neurologist Dr. Julius Korein. So, the possibility arises that one physician's "he's dead," may be another's "still has a spark, let's keep trying."

Cases illustrative of this point have occurred time and time again. One of the most noteworthy is the story of Sp/4 Jacky C. Bayne of the U.S. Army's 196th Light Infantry Brigade. In the summer of 1967, near Chu Lai, Vietnam, Bayne's police dog stepped on a mine. Shrapnel tore into the twenty-two-year-old soldier. When he arrived at a field hospital, physicians could find no pulse, no breathing, and no audible heartbeat.

Army physicians had worked on Bayne for about forty-five minutes, applying cardiac massage and artificial respiration. Readings from an electrocardiograph showed no heart activity. Clinically, physicians believed, the soldier was dead. Bayne's story could well have ended here—for thousands of GIs it probably has—but it was only the beginning of Bayne's second life.

For several hours he lay at Graves Registration. When an embalmer finally began the cutdown on his groin to expose the soldier's femoral artery, where embalming fluid would be injected, he noticed a faint pulse. Bayne's body was dispatched to a nearby hospital where a feverish resuscitation effort and blood transfusions confirmed the embalmer's discovery. This time resuscitation revived him.

After recuperation Bayne returned home. "He says the Lord brought him back from Vietnam," his mother reported. Although the young man had sustained some brain damage, some impaired function, he was far from dead.

At the time, Army doctors insisted that the South Carolinian's grim case was a "rarity." Signs of death, they said, are usually too clear to be mistaken by experienced doctors.

39

Dr. Korein carries this thought a step further when he notes that inherent in the diagnosis of death, only one type of error is permissible. "One may diagnose a patient as 'alive,' who is in fact 'dead.' It is not permissible, however, to make a diagnosis of death when the patient may be 'alive.' "

In an effort to slice through some of the problems inherent in the diagnosis of death by different physicians, Dr. Vincent J. Collins of Chicago's Cook County Hospital, in 1968, suggested a score card for death at the annual meeting of the American Medical Association. The Collins scoring system suggests that life or death be based on five physical functions: heartbeat, brain function, nerve reflexes, breathing function, and circulatory function. Each is given a score of two points if normal, one point if extraordinary measures are needed to produce a response, and zero if a response cannot be produced. The score is to be totaled every fifteen minutes over a period of one to six hours.

A score of five or more is considered a sign of potential life, less than five, impending death. "An increasing score represents effective therapy and patient recovery; while a decreasing score represents failing therapy and deterioration," Dr. Collins said. "Such a scoring system also will help the physician to decide when efforts at resuscitation should be abandoned and thus permit a patient to die in peace and not in pieces," the physician declared.

Under the Collins system if the patient is to become a transplant donor, artificial resuscitation can be resumed after the patient has been pronounced dead by physicians.

Rather than being a totally new idea and concept, the score card system was actually more of a summary or codification of medical opinion. It has never caught on because, in the average physician's practice of medicine, scoring systems and sophisticated machinery are rarely used to determine death. Each physician keeps his own score card on each patient, in his head.

The chief of medicine at one Midwestern hospital explains, "We'll put a person on a respirator, hook him up to an electrocardiograph (ECG.) If there is no motion on the ECG, and the heart is stopped, for even thirty seconds, and the patient has fixed dilated pupils, we don't even want to bring him back. He may live for another twelve hours as a vegetable, but that's not life, you don't have a person, but a biological preparation primed by machines."

No matter what the formalities or proclamations by august bodies, and no matter what use is made of complex machines, the physician will always be called upon to make life and death decisions. Two Minnesota physicians, Dr. A. Mohandas and Dr. Shelly Chou, argue in the *Journal of Neurology* that the clinical judgment of a neurosurgeon is more essential than the EEG reading in evaluating brain death. And Dr. M. F. A. Woodruff, vice president of England's Transplantation Society, doesn't think the revised criteria for defining death are in order at all. "In addition to the proposed new definition [brain death] being inconsistent with the views of ordinary men and women, its acceptance would necessitate the introduction of a new term to indicate that a body could be buried, unless of course . . . we are prepared to contemplate burying people while their hearts are still beating," Dr. Woodruff has said.

Woodruff does believe that circumstances do exist under which the life-sustaining machines should be turned off; but, he says, "let us adhere to the commonsense notion that while death will certainly ensue it does not take place the moment the switch is turned off."

The controversy will not come to an abrupt halt. All that can be hoped for at present and in the near future is that the persons who are in a position to make life and death decisions will keep themselves informed of theological and legal thinking as well as current medical practice.

"Medical science," suggests Dr. Hannibal Hamlin, "should strive to obtain practical agreement from church and law on the recognition of death as it affects the vital organs that govern the total organism, notwithstanding the persistent semantic and multilingual difficulties for formulating a definition satisfactory to all concerned."

The dialogue regarding criteria for the determination of death must continue, and the public must be kept informed to a greater extent than ever before. As Harvard's Dr. Beecher has said, "To dismiss the new definition of death is to dismiss meaningful thought about the cost, the loss in lives of salvageable men. A new era is at hand; for the first time, the human body of the newly dead has great potential usefulness."

> "Whatsoever ye would that men should
> do to you, do ye even so to them."
>
> Matthew 7:12

2

TRANSPLANTS

You Can Take It with You

Over the past few thousand years civilized man has developed the habit of putting a price on everything, especially things whose intangible values are difficult to comprehend. The value of museums, hospitals, great research centers is often figured exclusively in net financial terms, even though their true worth eludes such concrete evaluation. Art, coin, and antique collectors are constantly queried about their collections, "How much is it worth?"

The attempt to define in terms of money is all too often extended to human beings. How much does he earn? How much does he owe? How much is he worth?

How much *is* a person worth? Is it the $28,845.83 Mike Kasperak paid, for hospital and medical care, to have his heart replaced by Stanford surgeon Dr. Norman Shumway? Is it the $1,000 or more that a family pays for maternity, prenatal, and delivery expenses for a new child? Could it be the $3,000 to $7,500 paid on the adoption black market in California for prime white babies in perfect condition? The cost of life for a person with severe kidney ailments, who needs artificial dialysis, is between

43

$20,000 and $40,000 per year. Is that the cost of a human life?

Some years ago high school biology teachers estimated for curious students—who invariably asked the question—that all of the chemicals in the human body would bring something like $1.12 on the retail market. With inflation the figure probably has risen to about $3.50. But whatever the absolute cash value of a human body, it is basically the same for all mankind. Prostitute, gambler, murderer, bank president, literary genius (or critic); each person's body is made up of essentially the same chemical parts. A few grams of this, a few liters of that; minute traces of many precious elements and lots of some that aren't so precious.

Yet there is more to the human body than a few chemical elements and compounds. Something that nobody has been successful at valuing—on a realistic basis—for the retail market. That commodity is the life spirit. French philosopher Henri Bergson described it as *l'élan vital,* "the vital glow," what separates man from other living creatures on earth.

It cannot be man's living body, which is weaker than the ape's, can be outsoared by the eagle, outrun by the cheetah, and outswum by the fish, that separates him from the rest of the animal world. It is his brain alone. His ability to carry out the abstract processes of thought.

It is the manifestation of this special evolutionary inheritance that in each individual helps to determine what and who he will be. These, however, are factors over which man has no control at present. Except by way of heredity, the genetic "crap game," man cannot will his personality, intelligence, or physique to his descendants.

Other bequests allow man more control. When a person is able to accumulate financial wealth or material treasures during his lifetime, he often claims to derive special pleasure from the knowledge that he will be able to transfer such wealth—plus, perhaps, power and position—to his offspring. Throughout history man has taken great pride in his legacies to those who will survive. The legacies of the wealthy—passed from generation to generation—may be jewels, art treasures, or money.

But what of all the people who would like to bequeath

great gifts, titles, or power, but haven't the means? The opportunity for all individuals to leave something of true worth has arisen only in the past few decades. The platitude of not being able to take it with you just doesn't stand up any more; and it is not because we have begun to carry material wealth to the grave—as did the Egyptian pharaohs—or to any new afterlife. There now exists the possibility of giving ever-more precious gifts to succeeding generations—literally, the gift of life. We are only beginning to learn its worth.

The still mysterious substance of life has always been valued to a degree. It is only recently, however, with the surge in organ and tissue transplantation and the increasingly intense quest for medical knowledge, that the gift of life has become a possibility. Man can now, with a realistic hope of making a substantial contribution, bequeath his body, all or parts of it, for use in transplantation surgery, research, or dissection and study by medical students.

Transplant surgery began more than five thousand years ago when the Egyptians and Hindus performed skin grafts to restore noses destroyed by syphilis. Since then myriad tissues and organs have been transplanted. These include whole blood, blood vessels, bone, bone marrow, cartilage, tendons, skin, nerves, and parts of the eye. In addition more than 5,000 kidneys, 100 livers, 25 lungs, 160 hearts, as well as some glands have been transplanted with varying degrees of success.

In February of 1969, a fifty-seven-year-old New Yorker, whose name was never revealed, provided surgeons with the most abundant harvest to date from a single donor for organ transplants: a heart, two kidneys, a liver, and the corneas of both eyes. When the biological philanthropist died at New York Memorial Hospital for Cancer and Allied Diseases, his family made it clear that they, and he, wanted to make available as many organs as possible.

People from all walks of life have benefited from cadaver tissue. In 1968, in Columbia, Missouri, a convicted felon, working as a guard, was blinded by another inmate who was attempting a prison break. The man had his vision restored by a plastic cornea and a sclera—the tough, white outer covering of the eye—that had been preserved in an eye bank.

Another among thousands who have been helped by donated, tissue was a scientist named Dr. Belding H. Scribner of the University of Washington. Several years after Dr. Scribner's severely inpaired sight was restored to normal by a cornea transplant, he became the leader of a research team that developed another miracle of modern medical technology—the artificial kidney machine.

The transplantation of major organs, such as the heart, has received heavy criticism as premature. Though success has been limited, there has indeed been some success. Philip Blaiberg, Dr. Christiaan Barnard's second patient, who lived for 593 days after his operation, recalled, for example, "It used to be that I had to fight for every breath; I was never sure that I could take another. Every physical movement, every step walking, was hell. Now I feel refreshed. I can enjoy going down to the ocean—I've always loved the sea, you know. . . . I don't know how long my new ticker will work. But it will have given me precious days and weeks. And if I should snuff it tomorrow, I will at least do so in comfort."

The major stumbling block to successful transplant surgery remains the body's rejection of all foreign tissue except that which is matched almost perfectly. But physicians and scientists are regularly reporting new treatment modes or new information learned about the body's immune systems. The physiological problems, some have no doubt, will be overcome in the not too distant future. The crucial problem then will be: How can we supply enough organs for transplantation?

"Perhaps a third of future humanity will at some time during the course of their lives need an organ transplant," predicts Dr. Roy Walford, pathologist at the University of California at Los Angeles. "Terminal patients, victims of fatal accidents, condemned criminals who might be persuaded to will their healthy organs to society, and suicides, who number twenty-two thousand a year in the United States, all die anyway. It will be a tragic waste if their organs are not made available to patients whose lives could be prolonged."

The group of potential donors Walford mentions are all seemingly distant from the average man making a decision, long before the fact, to donate organs or body. The idea, of course, is that we should seriously consider donating our body parts long before we think we are approaching death. Accidents, after all, happen when they are least expected, often cutting a person down in the prime of life. Young, healthy organs from such situations are the most valuable to medical men.

The key question, however, remains: Do men really want to make their organs available? Man has long been ambivalent on the subject, as exemplified by the centuries-long struggle to establish dissection of the dead for medical purposes. Galen and other early anatomists were forced to base their anatomical conclusions on animal dissections and myths attributing various functions to certain body parts. This practice, predictably, led to inaccurate results. In spite of the fact that anatomical studies offered direct benefits to medicine, it was not until the Renaissance that medical experimenters were finally able to break through the taboos and actually examine the human body after death. Even the first enlightened anatomical laws of the nineteenth century permitted dissection only of the bodies of criminals and the poor. Thus arose the illicit trade of grave robbing in England and the United States. Enterprising thugs sought out information of impending deaths and funerals and as soon thereafter as possible visited the places of burial and dug up the bodies, which were sold to medical men at schools of anatomy.

About 1828 or 1829, in Edinburgh, Scotland, William Burke and a partner took it upon themselves to assist nature. They searched out the poor and the friendless, weakened them with liquor and lured them to their quarters. The victims were then suffocated—so as to leave no telltale marks on the body—and the bodies were sold to students of medicine. To this day the word *burking* has come to mean murder by suffocation or the act of hushing things up. Burke and his colleague killed some sixteen people and contributed them—for a price—to the most famous lecturers in the area. One prominent surgeon of the day was so pleased with the freshness and good condition of the bodies received that he often congratulated the "donors." Such escapades enraged the public and led to England's Anatomy Act of 1832, which put an end to the black market in bodies and regulated anatomy schools. Thereafter, only bodies that were not claimed could then be donated to medical science, and this is the tradition that has come down through the years.

Today public outrage has calmed toward dissection, but man is still not totally comfortable with the thought, especially in the United States. While an average of two million die in the United States each year, only about 20 per cent of the dead are even autopsied. A far smaller percentage offer their bodies for transplant or anatomical study in medical schools. This 20 per cent rate is extremely low when compared with statistics in other parts of the world. In Switzerland, for example, 80 per cent are autopsied, and in the Soviet Union the figure approaches 100 per cent. The differences can be attributed to several factors, one of which may be the traditional desire of attending physicians to spare the survivors a prolonged wait between the time of death and burial.

A few religious groups, most notably Orthodox Jews, have strongly opposed autopsies or any other form of human dissection. A part of Orthodox Jewish law calls for complete burial, based on the belief that the physical integrity of the body is a prerequisite for resurrection. (Some religious Jews have been known to save fingernail and hair clippings, as well as any organs removed during their lifetime, for burial at their death.) After an autopsy, however, all organs can be returned to the body for burial, thereby meeting the prescribed rules.

The present Orthodox Jewish view of autopsy was first formulated in 1776 by Rabbi Yecheskel Landau. His interpretation was that an autopsy could be performed if it is for the benefit of the *holeh shel-lifanenu,* "the sick person who is near us." In other words, the patient who may be helped by the autopsy of a dead person must be near in "time and place" to the body upon which the autopsy will be performed. Rabbis today have pointed out that in our modern world the concept can surely be extended. Today, for example, it is quicker to go from Paris to London by plane than it was to go by horse from one village to a nearby one in Rabbi Landau's time.

Citing another Jewish law, Great Britain's chief Rabbi

Immanuel Jakobovits adds that the performance of an autopsy in the case of saving a life, "is not only a matter of permission but of obligation and *mitzvah* ['good deed']."

Indeed, even though we now possess a fairly complete knowledge of man's anatomy, the most thorough physicians insist upon the necessity for autopsy. Autopsies, they say, are often the only way to determine the actual cause of death. In addition, autopsies often lead to new medical knowledge. If it weren't for autopsies, heart experts might still regard atherosclerosis as a disease of old age. It was through the post mortems of GIs killed in World War II and Korea that physicians first discovered signs of arterial clogging among teenagers. A colleague of heart specialist Dr. Paul Dudley White has reported that the famed physician "gets autopsies on all his patients even if their deaths seem straightforward—that's how the great men learn about disease."

In the past physicians have stressed repeatedly that there is an acute shortage of bodies donated for anatomical study. In the majority of institutions this is still the case, but during the early 1970s there has been an increase in cadaver donation, especially to the prestige medical schools such as Harvard. Dr. Duane Belt of Harvard's neighbor, Tufts Medical College, has noted, "The glamour of Harvard's name usually attracts more willed bodies than either Boston University or we do." So even after death Americans try to outdo their neighbors. The fact is, though, a single body donated for anatomical study to any of the nation's medical or dental schools may give two or more students the information they need to save literally thousands of lives during their careers.

Russell Fisher, M.D., Maryland's chief medical examiner, noted in 1969, "Currently there are not enough available bodies for optimum anatomical study in medical and dental schools; the ideal number would be five thousand annually. No reliable figures are available on the number needed for medical research. As the number of students and research investigators increases to meet growing demands, this need for bodies will continue to increase."

In 1970, Dr. Andrew Ramsay, professor of anatomy at Philadelphia's Jefferson Medical College, described the problem in his home state. "When I came here in 1936, there were 2,600 medical and dental students in Pennsylvania, and 734 cadavers available to them. Last year there were 5,200 students and only 340 cadavers. In recent years we've had additional requests for human tissue, from graduate students and research organizations, that we've been unable even to consider."

Dr. Ramsay recalled that in 1936, none of the cadavers reached medical schools through wills; all were unidentified dead persons or the bodies of those whose next of kin refused to accept the responsibility for disposing of them.

Today such situations are rare. Almost everyone has some kind of burial fund, even if it is nothing more than the Social Security allowance—set at a maximum of $255—for that purpose. Of the 340 cadavers Dr. Ramsay spoke of receiving in 1969, only 60 were those of persons who had specified the donation in their wills.

The gift of the human body for study or transplantation purposes is "the last act of unequivocal charity man is able to accomplish," states Dr. George Schreiner, past president of the National Kidney Foundation. "When living, generosity has to do with financial means. This, however, is really the most democratic and essential charity man can give."

One donor summed up his motivations this way for *Newsweek* magazine, "It is simple, logical, scientifically useful—and it is one foolproof way of beating the undertaker."

Another donor, David M. Cleary, medical writer for the *Philadelphia Evening Bulletin,* is a highly respected and astute observer of the medical profession. In a prize-winning article entitled, "I'm Giving My Body to Science," printed in 1970, Cleary explained some of the hows and whys of his action.

A few days ago I typed and signed this statement:
In the hope that I may help others, I hereby make this anatomical gift, to take effect upon my death.
I give my body to the Anatomical Board of the State of Pennsylvania for such uses, including transplantation of organs and anatomical study, as the board may deem appropriate, without restriction.

That simple declaration, also signed by two witnesses, is a legal document that brought me great peace of mind. I have a certified copy in my wallet, another where my survivors can reach it quickly, and a third was mailed to the office of the Anatomical Board. . . .

With that distribution of copies, I can be reasonably sure that:

—My survivors needn't go through the anguish of selecting a casket and making other funeral arrangements.

—Whatever memorial services are held won't be dominated by inert flesh from which my spirit has departed.

—And aside from whatever value my body may have in medical education and practice, the money that might otherwise be spent on a funeral will serve some useful purpose, such as education of a child or grandchild.

David Cleary's thoughts on the disposal of his own body after death are undoubtedly shared by many Americans. A large number, however, have no idea of how to go about making such a gift. Others wonder whether their religion allows such an action.

Actually the three major Western religions have not opposed transplantation from cadaver tissue except on the ground that scientists should show great care in two areas: first, that the donors be unquestionably dead, and second that the operations should be life-saving and never experimental on human beings.

In 1969 a task force on "Cardiac Replacement" reported to the National Heart and Lung Institute of the National Institutes of Health: "Although it is too early for the possible impact of vital organ transplantation to be fully realized by the various religious groups, experience to date in the Western world does not suggest any major incompatibility. While all of the possible questions have obviously not been raised or explored, theologians have agreed that transplants are 'morally licit' as a last resort to save a dying patient. . . . Cardiac and other organ transplantation has been held to be consistent with the beliefs of major religious groups."

Conservative Rabbi Bernard Lipnick of St. Louis goes a step further by saying, "If they are doing transplants to save the life of the individual recipient, rather than for experimentation or for long-run results, and if the donor is dead and the organ can be used to save a life, it is not only allowable, but under Jewish law it is a *mitzvah,* or good deed."

Actually until relatively recently, it was not easy for one to commit such a good deed and will his body or parts of it and be assured that his wishes would be carried out. Cumbersome and archaic laws surrounded circumstances by which such gifts could be made. Under common law, for example, individuals did not have the authority to make any kind of anatomical gift because the next of kin were entitled to possession of the body "in the same condition in which it was at the time of death."

Even early in 1969—fully a year and a half after the first successful human heart transplant, after hundreds of other body parts had been transplanted from cadavers— an instructor in forensic medicine at the University of Missouri Medical School told me that no matter what the overriding medical circumstances, "As a Missouri lawyer, I could not advise a physician in this state to do a major organ transplant from a nonliving donor simply because we do not have any precedents—statute or casewise—to say a physician could do it and not be confronted with possible liability."

Shortly thereafter, on May 28, 1969, Missouri's Governor Warren E. Hearnes signed into law the Uniform Anatomical Gifts Act, making organ donations for study and transplantation legal and relatively simple.

It was nearly a hundred years before, in 1881, that New York State enacted the first law to permit a living person to effectively authorize, in advance, a gift of his own body for medical purposes. In time, many other states passed statutes which gave the donation authority to the individual. And those actions—taken in some forty-four states— were commendable progress in their days. But they were not enough. Because each law was enacted by a different state legislature, under differing circumstances, no two were exactly the same and most of them differed greatly in their provisions. Thus there was always the question of whether the authorization of a gift made in one state would be valid in another. Delivery of donated bodies or organs across state lines involved legal complications which made it inadvisable even under the best circumstances. Federal law would not apply because matters pertaining to inheritance, death, and birth are responsibilities of the states.

Order was needed to settle the many legal questions. Hope came when the National Conference of Commissioners on Uniform State Laws, a standing group of experts on unifying and updating legislation for the states, agreed to draft a model anatomical donation law. Under the chairman, E. Blythe Stason, the committee met with representatives of the medical and legal professions and after a few years approved a model Uniform Anatomical Gift Act on July 20, 1968.

The basic provisions of the model UAGA are as follows:

1. Any person eighteen years or older may donate all or part of his body after death for transplantation, research, or placement in a tissue bank.
2. A donor's valid statement of gift supersedes the rights of others unless a state autopsy law prevails.
3. If a donor has not acted during his lifetime, his survivors, by a specific order of priority, may do so.
4. Physicians who accept anatomical gifts, relying in good faith on the documents, are protected from legal action.
5. Time of death must be determined by a physician not involved in the transplant.
6. The donor may revoke the gift, or it may be rejected.

Although, before the adoption of the UAGA, many states provided for one or more similar points, the UAGA brought it all together. In the incredibly short time of just over two years after the drafting and endorsement of the UAGA, it, or reasonably similar laws, were in effect in all fifty states. These state laws follow the model act in all major respects except for differences such as the age at which the donor can make a valid gift, the requirement of confidentiality, or the number of witnesses required.

While medical writer David Cleary felt it necessary to

compose a specific letter of intent, and have it notarized, the UAGA provides that an individual's donation need only be made by any written document, which "may be a card designated to be carried on the person."

The card must be signed by the donor and witnessed by two persons. The convenience of the card, of course, is that in situations where time is of the essence—where the donor is dead or close to it, and the existence of a will is unknown—physicians may go ahead with any procedures they deem necessary after death.

Some doctors speculate that in the future the simple cardboard card will evolve into an instrument similar to a credit card. On a small magnetic tape on the back of the card will be recorded all of the donor's pertinent biological data: blood and tissue types, age, medical history, etc. It will simply be a matter of feeding this information into a central computer center for the physician to quickly locate possible recipients for any tissues or organs.

Reliable statistics as to the number of Americans who have made arrangements to donate all or parts of their bodies to medical science are not available. A Gallup Poll in January 1968, shortly after the first heart transplant, estimated that seven of every ten Americans would be willing to give their hearts or other vital organs to science after death. However, estimates of the number of Americans who have actually made such arrangements range up to only two hundred thousand.

Voluntary health groups such as the National Kidney Foundation have distributed some two million Uniform Donor Cards. (For a free card write the National Kidney Foundation, 315 Park Avenue South, New York, New York 10010.) Nobody knows, however, exactly how many persons have signed and are carrying the cards.

If my own experiences are typical, I suspect that only one of every thirty to fifty donor cards is seeing active duty. When I first interviewed Dr. Schreiner at the National Kidney Foundation in 1970, I asked for several dozen extra donor cards to distribute to friends and colleagues who, I was sure, would be interested. To my surprise, none accepted.

"Who wants to think that far ahead?" one asked. Another said, "When I die they won't need my body." And so it went down the line, from boss to friend to mere acquaintance. Some laughed, some joked, some pretended not to hear. Some denied the importance of making such a commitment. But the fact is that I could not convince one person to accept, fill out, and carry one of the Uniform Donor Cards.

This general apathy is one reason that some eminent professionals have suggested that the UAGA is not liberal. enough. They suggest that the law should permit routine autopsy and other organ removal for medical purposes unless the subject or his next of kin has objected. Thus the responsibility would be placed directly on the patient or his next of kin to object, rather than on the physician to seek permission. Proponents argue that such a plan would cause far less mental trauma for the patient and family, and that the net gain would be much greater.

Such a proposal raises the question of who actually possesses the rights to a human body after death. If the responsibility for autopsy and organ removal goes to the state, then why should the state not assume all responsibilities for the corpse, including total burial expense? And what of those whose religion specifically forbids mutilation of the body after death, and whose next of kin may not be quickly available to make a decision? Certainly a middle ground can be reached. Perhaps no more is needed than massive public education campaigns combined with the existing laws.

Even with the publicity already received by the body-organ donation organizations, current resistance is not totally inexplicable. First of all, man denies his own mortality. Secondly, prejudice plays a part; as recently as World War II, for example, some people were shocked by blood transfusions—especially those that mixed Negro blood with white, or Jewish with gentile. Today, however, as a result of publicity campaigns that have stressed the number of lives saved, blood transfusions have become commonplace.

In the future the day may come when our fears, prejudices, and selfishness with regard to our own bodies after death will disappear. When that time comes, donor organs may be exchanged on an international basis according to need: An American may be kept alive with a Chinese liver, a Russian with an American kidney, or even an Israeli with the heart of an Egyptian.

When man willingly offers the gift of life to his fellow man, the world will benefit more than simply biologically.

"A time to be born and a time to die . . .
a time to kill and a time to heal."

Ecclesiastes 3:2–3

3

EUTHANASIA
Let There Be Death

Within a period of seven days early in 1972, judges in Milwaukee and New York made two life and death decisions in cases which were in their essence remarkably similar. The two judges, however, made opposite rulings concerning an individual's right to die.

The subject of the New York ruling was Clarence A. Bettman, a seventy-nine-year-old investment banker who was "factually incompetent." Over his wife's objections the court gave permission for surgeons at New York Hospital-Cornell Medical Center to implant a new battery in the pacemaker that maintained Bettman's heartbeat.

In Milwaukee, however, the court upheld that seventy-seven-year-old Mrs. Gertrude Raasch, who refused to sign papers authorizing the removal of her gangrenous leg, be allowed to die "in God's own peace." The Milwaukee case began to unfold when, on Friday, January 21, Walter G. Hardman, administrator of the city's Doctor's Hospital, came to Judge Sullivan's court and testified that Mrs. Raasch, who was scheduled for her third major operation in six weeks and her second in ten days, had refused to authorize the amputation which doctors said was necessary to save her life. Mrs. Raasch had spent the last seventeen years in and out of hospitals and nursing homes, had no living relatives, and already her leg had been amputated to mid-calf because of the gangrenous infection.

After hearing the testimony of the hospital official, Judge Sullivan said, "The court is in the position of determining . . . whether the lady shall live. This is because, according to physicians, unless the operation is performed at three o'clock, which is less than one hour from now, she will not live longer than this weekend."

The judge noted, however, that "It is not the prerogative of this court to make decisions for adult competent citizens, even decisions relating to life and death."

Before making his decision, Judge Sullivan sent an attorney to the hospital to determine whether Mrs. Raasch could be considered competent by the court. The attorney returned and said that Mrs. Raasch could not talk, but he had communicated with her by asking her to touch his hand in response to questions. He said that she indicated that she was in pain, but could understand him.

"When it came to the critical question, 'Do you wish to submit to further surgery?' she would just whimper and cry and not respond," he said.

Under Wisconsin State law, Judge Sullivan could not assign a guardian for the action unless the person was mentally incompetent or deficient, which, he ruled, Mrs. Raasch was not. So, on that day, Judge Sullivan denied the hospital's petition to perform further surgery on Mrs. Raasch.

The case received national publicity. Cards, letters, and telephone calls poured into Doctor's Hospital. One little girl wrote and asked if she could adopt Mrs. Raasch as her grandmother. A Houston housewife pleaded, "Is there anything at all I can do? I want to help but I feel so helpless."

By the following Monday, in spite of the earlier medical testimony, Mrs. Raasch was still alive. On that day Judge Sullivan received a telephone call from an acquaintance who told him that he "had a neighbor lady who knew Mrs.

Raasch personally and she felt that if she could talk to Mrs. Raasch she would change her mind about the operation."

The "neighbor lady," Gertrude Krause, had been the administrator of a nursing home at which Mrs. Raasch had previously stayed. She told Judge Sullivan that she herself had called the hospital and told them that she wished to speak to Mrs. Raasch. Faced with dozens of calls concerning the case, the hospital dismissed her request and "hung up on her."

Because this new factor had entered the situation, Judge Sullivan reopened the case the following morning and went to the hospital with Mrs. Krause. At 8:00 A.M. the two entered the hospital room.

"Mrs. Raasch was a very small woman, very thin, but very bright," Judge Sullivan recalled. "Her eyes were opened and she recognized Mrs. Krause immediately and I was introduced as a friend. Mrs. Raasch tried to talk but the words wouldn't come out. She responded to questions by shaking her head or nodding it. She recognized the names of mutual acquaintances. Mrs. Krause took out a picture of a little Yorkshire terrier that Mrs. Raasch used to play with and she immediately recognized the dog and smiled."

And then Mrs. Krause said, "Gertrude, why don't you have the operation?"

Mrs. Raasch closed her eyes and shook her head vigorously. Mrs. Krause offered to go up to surgery with her friend and remain with her afterward. Mrs. Raasch's face tensed up and, said the judge, "it was obvious that she didn't want any more surgery."

In Judge Sullivan's final statement on the matter he said that there was "absolutely no evidence of incompetence on the part of Mrs. Raasch except that she is too weak to talk. . . . I'm positive we're doing the right thing—we will leave Mrs. Raasch to depart in God's own peace."

Later, discussing the case, Judge Sullivan said that the major legal question he had to determine was "Is the lady incompetent? If she is not incompetent I have no right to appoint a guardian. As far as I am concerned this was an easy decision to make. Assuming I had found her incompetent this would have raised a more hairy problem. How far do you want the doctors to go with an incompetent person?"

This was exactly the "hairy" situation faced by New York State Supreme Court Justice Gerald P. Culkin when he appointed a guardian for Clarence Bettman and authorized the hospital to "perform whatever medical and surgical procedures" were "necessary to protect or sustain the health or life" of the man.

According to an attending surgeon at the hospital, the authorization for the operation was requested because Bettman was factually incompetent, unaware of his condition, incapable of making the decision, and because his wife had rejected numerous requests by the hospital for permission to perform the operation.

Mrs. Bettman was angry about the court order and the hospital's decision to perform the minor surgery necessary to replace the battery in her husband's pacemaker. "I resisted as long as I could and then I gave in," she said.

"What has he got to live for? Nothing. He knows nothing, he has no memory whatsoever. He is turning into a vegetable. Isn't death better?" Mrs. Bettman asked.

Four months after his pacemaker batteries were replaced Clarence Bettman was in about the same condition as at the time of his operation, "resting quietly" at a Connecticut nursing home.

The Rev. Dr. Joseph Fletcher has pointed out that the old-fashioned question faced by physicians was, "May we morally do anything to put people out of hopeless misery?" But the issue has shifted, and now the question is, "May we morally omit doing any of the ingenious things we *could* do to prolong people's suffering?"

However stated, the problem of whether we should prolong useless life (or painful dying) has come to be represented by a single word: *euthanasia.*

The immediate association that comes to mind upon reading or hearing this word is "mercy killing," but advocates maintain they are really referring to the word's literal meaning, "a good or happy death," "an easy and painless death." The word *euthanasia* comes from the Greek *eu,* meaning "well" and *thanatos,* meaning "death." The semantic entanglements over the implied meaning are the center of much of the controversy over the subject. The

Euthanasia Society and the Euthanasia Educational Fund, groups that promote the "good death" doctrine, have considered a name change—centering, perhaps, around "Death with Dignity"—because of adverse reactions to the word *euthanasia*. A good deal of resistance to the word today is probably due to man's revulsion over the Nazi war crimes, many of which were performed by physicians misappropriating the word *euthanasia* as a cloak for their murders.

"It's a common misunderstanding that we advocate mercy killing, but actually, mercy killing is the complete antithesis of what we seek. The question is not one of killing people. It's the question of letting them die," says Jerome Nathanson, chairman of the board of the New York Society for Ethical Culture and a proponent of euthanasia.

Others interested in promoting the idea of the "good death" may join the nonprofit Euthanasia Educational Fund, or its lobbying partner, the Euthanasia Society. The two groups, staffed mainly by volunteers, share a cramped office on West Fifty-seventh Street in Manhattan. In 1969 the combined membership in the organizations was six hundred. In late 1971 there were more than six thousand members, and the lists are growing rapidly. Any person who contributes to the fund automatically becomes a member, and because many of the contributors are elderly and retired, there is no minimum contribution required.

The first Euthanasia Society was founded in England in 1935 by a physician who wanted to promote legislation to "make the act of dying more gentle." The American society was founded in 1938, but its educational arm was formed only a few years ago. Its aims are:

To promote consideration by professionals and the public of the ultimate reality of death.

To allay fears surrounding this whole subject by opening it up to free and honest discussion.

To examine procedures, teaching and attitudes toward patients in terminal illness.

To seek ways of humanizing death, and to work toward creating a climate of public opinion to this end.

The fund finances studies and seminars on euthanasia for physicians, clergymen, social workers, nurses, and lawyers. A newsletter and educational booklets are published and distributed to members and others seeking information. Thousands of individuals write each month to the groups' headquarters, either asking for information or simply expressing their own opinions. Few negative letters are received.

A California man wrote that "No S.O.B. on earth is going to keep me from making the trip promptly." A Texas man noted, "I thoroughly agree with your view that if there is no reasonable expectation of my recovering from physical or mental disability, [that] I be allowed to die"; and a Philadelphia professional man wrote that he appreciated "your efforts in taking on our culture's uptight relationship to death and dying."

Another letter—not uncommon in content—came from a lawyer in the South who wrote, "I am handling an estate where there was no hope for the deceased to live, but through strenuous efforts of several doctors he was kept breathing for a long period. The hospital and doctors' bills exceeded $25,000 and impoverished the estate."

A grandmother of three wrote from her home in the Midwest that she was "seventy years old and in good health, but I don't want to suffer when doctors feel it is a losing battle. I don't want the ones I love to witness that kind of suffering."

The letters come in all forms, typed by secretaries or scrawled on scraps of note paper. They are from the uneducated as well as the professional, from students and grandparents, nuns, clergymen, and laymen. The vast majority of them share the opinion expressed by Mrs. George C. Barclay, a seventy-one-year-old volunteer for the two groups, who says, "We should have a reverence for life, yes. But we should have the right to die with dignity. You shouldn't drag out a good life."

Euthanasia is an ancient practice. Geographer Strabo, in the first century B.C., wrote that the elderly people on the Greek isle of Cos, having outlived their usefulness to society, would gather at an annual banquet to drink a lethal poison. In Massilia, modern Marseilles, one of the oldest Greek colonies, a death potion was made available in a public repository for the use of any citizen who could justify before the Senate his motive—usually illness, sorrow, or disgrace—which led him to desire death.

In one of his late works Cicero asked, "What reason is there for us to suffer? A door is open for us—death, eternal refuge where one is sensible of nothing."

And in the *Republic*, Plato described the ideal physician as one who, through personal experience, was familiar with disease and urged the profession to "minister to better natures, giving health both of soul and body. . . . Those who are diseased in their body they will leave to die; and the corrupt and incurable souls, they will put an end to themselves."

With the rise in Christianity in the first three centuries A.D., the approach to euthanasia and suicide underwent a complete change. From the beginning the Apostle Paul argued against any form of self-destruction, and he was followed by St. Augustine and other fathers of the church.

Although the opinion of the church remained clear, medical opinion on the subject was never fully crystallized during ancient times. Of course, medicine was not then sufficiently advanced in its life-prolonging powers to warrant a great deal of practical interest in the subject. But as the science advanced, so did the controversy.

Writing in 1880, the German physician Rohlfs regarded euthanasia as such an important topic that he referred to it as "obstetrics of the soul," and considered it a medical discipline in itself.

Many who are today opposed to the "good death" cite the Oath of Hippocrates (which he probably did not actually write himself) as an indictment of the medical practice of euthanasia in any form. Others more favorably disposed to euthanasia argue that Hippocrates lived some twenty-five hundred years ago; he could scarcely have visualized modern machines which can supplant the vital efforts of lungs or heart, and could never have predicted the ethical questions their use poses. Still a third group argues that the Oath remains valid, but differences can arise through interpretation.

The first passage of the Oath that concerns us states, "I will follow that method of treatment which, according to my ability and judgment, I consider for the benefit of my patients and abstain from whatever is deleterious and wrong."

Dr. Vincent Collins, anesthesiologist at Chicago's Cook County Hospital, asked in a 1962 article in the *Saturday Evening Post,* "How can it be judged to be to the benefit of a patient to cheat him of peace while being powerless to restore him to consciousness? Only a person who thinks of human life in terms of a senseless specimen of protoplasm in a test tube can see any merit in such a course. After all, consciousness alone means life to human beings."

Another phrase in the Oath states, "I will neither give a deadly drug to anybody, if asked for, nor will I make a suggestion to this effect." Many scholars believe that this provision was aimed specifically at preventing conspiracy, so that physicians would not enter into poisoning plots, which were fairly frequent in the political rivalries of the day.

Rev. Fletcher notes that the Oath contains no statements about making "the preservation of life the *summum bonum,* 'the highest good.' " To the contrary, he says, Hippocrates was a case-minded physician who would not attach himself blindly to absolutes or generalities. One of Hippocrates' favorite maxims was "Life is short and art is long, the occasion fleeting, experience fallacious and judgment difficult."

Hippocrates knew, says Fletcher, "the relativity of decision and made no attempt to establish its difficult demands by escaping into arbitrary and irresponsible absolutes."

In today's medical, legal, and theological circles it is generally accepted that there are two basic forms of euthanasia: direct (or positive) and indirect (or negative). Direct euthanasia is defined as a deliberate action to shorten a life. Injecting air into a dying person's bloodstream and causing an air embolism, for example, would be a direct euthanasia, a positive action shortening life, a "mercy killing." As current laws stand, this type of action is considered murder. Still, many feel that it should be permissible.

Indirect euthanasia is a much more common, and complicated, action which, while difficult to prove as murder, might be vulnerable to malpractice suits. In indirect euthanasia death is not induced, rather it is permitted. In other words, death is accomplished through the omission of an act or acts rather than by commission. Indirect euthanasia can take one of three forms: the administration of a fatal painkiller, halting treatments that prolong the life of the patient, or altogether withholding treatment.

It is interesting to note that a number of years ago Rev. Fletcher attempted to coin a new term, *antidysthanasia,* for this indirect ending of life. At the time he said that euthanasia referred only to the direct inducing of an easy death. Since that time, however, the eminent theologian has concluded that this division of terms is a mistake. "The problem of a good death is at stake in every and all forms. Nothing is won by playing the word game, and those who are locked in and committed to opposing euthanasia are not really being helped by linguistic escape hatches. . . . Nothing will be gained by trying to soften or truncate the issue, even though it is admittedly complex and freighted with emotion."

Along the same lines Dr. Robert Morrison suggests, in the journal *Science,* that "the more one thinks of actual situations . . . the more one wonders if there is a valid distinction between allowing a person to die and hastening the downward course of life. . . . The intent appears to be the same in the two cases, and it is the intent that would seem to be significant. . . . To use an analogy with mathematics, subtracting one from one would seem to be the same as not adding one to zero."

It is only in the last few decades that man has acquired the medicine and the technology that enables him to ease pain and suffering humanely and also to increase the average human's life span from 47.3 years in 1900 to 70.8 in 1970. Perhaps, however, we have learned to prolong and extend lives too well. Have we begun to pay too much attention to the quantity of human life and too little to its quality? In our haste to improve life-sustaining and resuscitative technologies have we gone too far? Have we reached the point where life itself may be more terrifying than death?

In January 1957, in the *Atlantic Monthly,* an article appeared under the title, "A New Way of Dying." The anonymous author wrote:

65

There is a new way of dying today. It is the slow passage via modern medicine. If you are very ill modern medicine can save you. If you are going to die it can prevent you from doing so for a very long time. . . . We cannot inquire from the dead what they have felt about this deterrent. As they fight for spiritual release, and are constantly dragged back by modern medicine to try again, does their agony augment? To those who stand and watch, this seems like a ghastly imposition against God's Will be done—this incredible battle between spirit and medicine.

Spirit versus medicine. The battle has been and will continue to be fought. Modern medicine has reached the point where control over disease is hardly questioned. There have been outstanding successes: Smallpox, typhus, cholera, polio, all scourges of the past, have succumbed. But new battles lie ahead and new frontiers await opening. Still, most of today's major moral concerns have been elicited by the rapid advances in the control of life and health. Each time a victory is gained, new ethical questions arise. Each advance in the capability of medicine increases the responsibility for decision making. Abortion, fertility and birth control, test-tube babies, new methods of creating pain or pleasure, the control of thought, and the actual creation of life itself, all demand new ways of thinking. Man has begun to learn to cope with the possibilities and the facts. Now the resuscitators, kidney machines, artificial body parts, and the actual transplantation of organs from one human being to another force us to take responsibility not only for the control of birth and the control of life, but also the control of death.

"With some justification," argues Dr. Frank J. Ayd, Jr., editor of the *Medical-Moral Newsletter,* "an increasing number of doctors have voiced objections to the 'obscenity of modern dying—a ritual sacrifice on the altar of technology.' Some have gone so far as to inform their own physicians and relatives and to carry on their person a card stating 'I do not wish to be resuscitated. I want to die with dignity—and forever.'"

Is it possible that twentieth-century man, who basks in the glory of his achievements, so far has been guilty of misusing his glorious creations? Has he reached the point where the healers, the technologists, and the rest of us are subject to Sir Theodore Fox's famous rebuke: "We shall have to learn to refrain from doing things merely because we know how to do them"?

The classic deathbed scenes familiar to us through our art and literature are rare today. Formerly, man died at home, surrounded by relatives and friends. He was aware of approaching death and he prepared for it. Today, however, the intimate circle of family and friends seldom gathers at the home of a dying loved one to exchange final words of love, faith, and wisdom. The deaths of Washington and Lincoln, great men of our country's past, stand in contrast with the death of Dwight D. Eisenhower, who was not permitted to die so easily. A pacemaker, a defibrillator, and modern drugs helped prolong the former president's life through an amazing series of crises—seven heart attacks, intestinal blockage, and pneumonia.

Today most deaths occur in the hospital. Death is no longer a peaceful, though grievous, occasion enveloped by the warmth of familial feelings. Now when man dies his mind is fogged by drugs, he is alone, surrounded and sustained only by the hum of machines. Family members often resent being deprived of the chance to share life's waning moments with their loved ones; and the dying surely must wonder why after years of shared sorrows and joys they cannot be allowed to face the greatest of all crises with their families.

Certainly, if a terminally ill person longs for the relief that only death can offer he should be permitted to have, at the very least, assurances that his life will not be needlessly prolonged. Rev. Fletcher warns that "the white coat of medical care takes on a darker more threatening hue, an uglier symbolism. We are discovering that saving life is not always saving people. And that death may not always be an enemy to be fought off, but sometimes a friend to be helped and invited."

Any individual who has ever visited the terminal ward of a hospital and heard a house physician mutter, in black humor, that he had to "go water the vegetables in their beds," would have to agree. Why should resuscitation or needless prolonging of life be allowed to extend or renew a patient's suffering? "To sacrifice human dignity at the time of death or to make the process of dying a burden upon the living is not in the highest tradition of medicine, nor is it justified in the humanist tradition," Dr. W. N. Hubbard, former dean of the University of Michigan Medical School, has said.

But if humanity and compassion for the dying are not reason enough, there is the matter of economics, the shameful waste of hospital space, manpower, and money involved in special care when, by disease, age, or accident, the body's usefulness has been ended.

All of this is not to suggest that we should shift our focus, even for a moment, from the welfare of the patient. Nor do we imply that decisions to "pull the plug," or not try another drug, or machine, are simple. The dilemma is not a totally new one, though it has been compounded ten thousand times in recent years. Physicians are trained to keep patients alive. A cured patient is a success, a dying patient a failure.

It becomes clear, however, that physicians must distinguish between treating primarily their own anxieties, and deciding what is best for the patient. The belief that the death of a patient represents a personal failure can lead to the unrestrained use of artificial life-support systems. The truly sensitive physician must learn to understand and accept the fact that death, inevitably, is a part of life.

"Our medical students," comments Dr. Walter Sackett of Florida, "are still being taught this philosophy [of keeping individuals alive, regardless] with little regard to the meaningfulness of the state of life. We really need to indoctrinate our neophyte physicians in a more humane theory of preservation of life."

Yet as an editorial in the physicians' newspaper *Medical Tribune* has pointed out, there are dilemmas in determining just what humane treatment is.

From time to time we are criticized for the overly dramatic and desperate treatment of moribund patients—for so surrounding the poor soul with infusions, oxygen, pressor amines, residents and attendings that the relatives can barely have a glimpse of him amid a forest of equipment. The effort is sourly criticized as "a prolongation of death," not of life, and a plea is made for the dignity of a patient's last hours when he ought to be allowed to die in peace. . . . [However], heroic treatment can succeed. As a result, quite a few "moribund" patients afterward stride out of the hospital in defiance of any reasonable judgment at the time of admission.

A convenient example is offered by Dr. Christiaan Barnard in his autobiography *One Life*. Dr. Barnard wrote that as a young intern at South Africa's Groote Schuur Hospital, he was very close to committing euthanasia on a woman who was in great agony from terminal cancer. As Dr. Barnard held a syringe filled with a lethal dose of morphine over the dying woman's arm, he suddenly decided that he was "violating not only the laws of social man, but also my own most personal ethic." The next day, Dr. Barnard relates, the woman rallied and lived for several years with the disease in an arrested state.

Even physicians, after years of experience, may not be able to determine whether treatment will be successful 100 per cent of the time. When an accident or drowning or shock causes the heart to stop, there is often reason to believe that the patient can be restored quickly enough to rule out damage to his brain. But if death results from a chronic disease, there is usually little hope of reversing it. It is frequently possible, though, to stave off total biological death, or even total brain death, by artificial means. As noted in an earlier chapter, however, what was once a living, thinking person can be reduced to little more than a biological preparation. Should the person have the right to die in such a situation? May he kill himself or request assistance in doing so? If he is not able to make such a request should the family be asked their opinion? If the family is not available, should the life or death decision be reserved for a group of physicians or perhaps a single one?

Many have warned of the implications inherent in leaving this kind of decision to any single person, especially the physician. One reason given is simply that it is a doctor's job to save, not take lives. Dr. Frank Ayd argues that it would be "very dangerous indeed to empower doctors to kill, on demand, the patients they cannot cure." There is no question that it would be a difficult task for the conscientious and thoughtful physician to determine at what state of an illness a patient would qualify for euthanasia. What criteria could be drawn? Would a seventy-year-old qualify for euthanasia at the same stage of disease as a twenty-year-old, or a baby born with serious congenital birth defects? Would a genius be allowed to die at the same point as a moron?

The question is complicated further by the fact that it would be difficult to determine whether the patient was fully aware when he made his request. Some still argue that any person who wishes to die is mentally unstable or incompetent. In certain states any person who commits, or attempts to commit, suicide is by law automatically declared *non compus mentis*. But does a dying person actually have to be insane to want to end his misery by wishing his own life to cease? When suicide, or suspected suicide, becomes a possibility, it can affect insurance settlements since many life insurance policies have clauses which render them void in the event of suicide. In the case of a person suffering from terminal cancer would this be fair? If the individual is not to be permitted to make certain decisions concerning his own life and death, who is? "It is better," says Dr. Ayd, "for the community to tie the hands of a good doctor by refusing to legalize the voluntary euthanasia, in order to restrain an unscrupulous one from violating the rights of the individual."

In an article in the physician's magazine *Medical Counterpoint,* Dr. Ray V. McIntyre, a family practitioner in Kingfisher, Oklahoma, also questions the choice of the physician as the administrator of euthanasia. "It is thought-provoking to consider the safeguards thought to be desirable in a legal system of euthanasia," he says, and notes that most plans call for the physician to carry out the wishes of a dying patient. "Since present legal executions use professional executioners, it seems to be a cultural anomaly to appoint a physician trusted by his patient to this lethal role."

On the other hand, the patient must also trust his physician not to put him through unnecessary pain, agony, and stress. As early as 1798 British physician Dr. J. Ferriar cautioned that the physician "should not torment his patient with unavailing attempts to stimulate the dissolving system, from the idle vanity of prolonging the flutter of the pulse for a few more vibrations: if he cannot alleviate his situation, he will protect his patient against every suffering. . . . When things come to the last and the act of dissolution is imminent . . . he should be left undisturbed."

Ferriar's philosophy has been reaffirmed by American courts several times. A decision similar to the one in the Gertrude Raasch case, discussed earlier in this chapter, was made in 1971 by a Florida judge in the case of Carmen Martinez, a seventy-two-year-old Cuban who had for two months been suffering from a fatal form of hemolytic anemia.

The treatment keeping Mrs. Martinez alive involved painful surgical incisions, called cutdowns, into her already battered veins so that an almost continual blood transfusion could be given. "Please don't torture me any more," she begged her physician, Dr. Rolando Lopez.

Faced with the dilemma of being charged with aiding and abetting a suicide on one hand, or treating a patient against her will on the other, Dr. Lopez sought counsel from the courts.

Circuit Court Judge David Popper also faced a dilemma because United States law has not really resolved the issue. Unable to find any precedent which would serve as a guide, the judge concluded that the law clearly opposes suicide, but just as clearly, a person "has the right not to be tortured."

Judge Popper said, "I can't decide whether she should live or die; that's up to God. . . . A person has a right not to suffer pain. A person has the right to live or die in dignity."

The judge's ruling was that Mrs. Martinez could not be forced to accept any treatment that was painful. The transfusions were stopped, and a day later Mrs. Martinez was dead. When he was informed of the death the judge declared, "I hope she died in peace." He refused further comment on the ground that it would be unethical of him to comment on a case which could still have been appealed to settle the "death with dignity" question for the future.

The same year, the Supreme Court of New Jersey ruled

that there is no "constitutional right to die." The decision stemmed from legal action taken by the John F. Kennedy Memorial Hospital to obtain authority for an operation and blood transfusion for a twenty-two-year-old girl whose religious beliefs forbade transfusions. The girl, Delores Heston, was a Jehovah's Witness.

She was severely injured in a car accident; hospital personnel said she was in a state of shock upon admittance. Physicians were convinced that, unless they performed surgery on her ruptured spleen without delay, she would die. They said blood transfusion was an imperative part of such an operation.

The girl's mother, Jane Heston, refused to sanction the transfusion and instead signed a release freeing the hospital and medical personnel from liability. The hospital then sought a court order seeking the appointment of a guardian for the patient. The court granted this, the guardian gave permission for the operation and transfusions, the operation was carried out, and the patient survived.

"It could hardly be said," the high court asserted, "that thus to save someone from himself violated a right under the Constitution, subjecting the rescuer to civil or penal consequences."

While the judge pointed out that attempted suicide was a crime under common law as well as in New Jersey statutes, the young woman's counsel argued that there was a difference between passively submitting to death and actively seeking it.

The court replied that if the state could interrupt one method of self-destruction, it could with equal authority interfere with the other. "The solution sides with life," the court added, "the conservation of which is a matter of state interest."

Because of the possibilities of such diverse rulings, lawyers and legislators in both the United States and England have attempted to deal with the question of the good death. The eminent British jurist Glanville Williams notes that under present law even voluntary euthanasia would be generally regarded as "suicide in the patient who consents and murder in the doctor who administers.

"Even on a lenient view, most lawyers would say that it could not be less than manslaughter in the doctor, the punishment for which, according to the jurisdiction and the degree of manslaughter, can be anything up to imprisonment for life," Williams explains.

At the same time, the law professor argues that some persons have long thought that the merciful extinction of life is permissible morally and even mandatory when "performed upon a dying patient with his consent and is the only way of relieving his suffering. . . . A man is entitled to demand the release of death from hopeless and helpless pain, and a physician who gives this release is entitled to moral and legal absolution for his act."

The implication here is that a person has the right, under certain circumstances, to have his life shortened. Dr. Leon Kass, writing in *Science,* disagrees. "Strictly speaking, I doubt if we could establish the *right* to be mercifully killed. Rights imply duties, and I doubt that we can make killing the duty of a friend or loved one."

Questioning Dr. Kass, however, one reader of the respected journal, R. I. Wolfe, wrote that "It is not a question of making it a duty; the duty is there."

Wolfe's rebuttal continued: "As Kass's words appeared in print, my wife's mother was entering the last few weeks of a long and agonized decline into death. Every time we visited her she asked (when she was lucid) '*Why* don't you help me die?' She was accusing us, and rightly, of not doing our duty by one whom we loved and respected."

Such situations are not unusual these days. The commonlaw tradition upon which today's legal system is based, however, makes no accommodations, for it is not founded on the precepts of modern medicine, but on the practice of medicine years ago.

On the other hand, no doctor in the United States has ever been jailed or had his license permanently revoked on a euthanasia charge.

One of the rare cases of a physician being prosecuted for mercy killing either here or in Great Britain occurred in 1949, when Dr. Hermann N. Sander of Manchester, New Hampshire, admitted to injecting air into the blood vessels of a fifty-nine-year-old cancer patient. The doctor had dictated his admission into the patient's hospital record.

Dr. Sander entered the courtroom charged with first-degree murder—which carried life imprisonment as a maximum penalty. At his trial, however, Dr. Sander was acquitted by the jury because it could not be established that his patient was actually alive at the time of the air injection, or even that the air bubble killed her. The only penalty was a temporary suspension of the physician's license.

Other cases have occurred in which the defendants were relatives of the deceased and not physicians. In some cases convictions have been handed down, but in others the individuals have been acquitted.

In 1927 in England there was a case in which a man had drowned his fatally ill child. The father had nursed his daughter faithfully, but one day after staying up with his child all the night before, he could no longer endure her suffering and he put the girl out of her misery. On the bench was Mr. Justice Branson who, in the course of his summation, said: "It is a matter which gives food for thought when one comes to consider that, *had this poor child been an animal instead of a human being, so far from there being anything blameworthy in the man's action in putting an end to its suffering, he would actually have been liable to punishment if he had not done so*" [italics added].

The jury's verdict: not guilty of murder.

Consider the possibility that a less compassionate judge might have been on the bench, and the equally likely possibility that the jury could have been less thoughtful in considering the case.

In 1936, in the House of Lords, a bill seeking to permit voluntary euthanasia, under certain circumstances and with certain safeguards, was introduced. Although the bill was rejected thirty-five to fourteen, it kept open the possibility for submission of similar bills in future. Discussing the bill, Lord Dawson of Penn observed that the ethics of the situation had to do with the "value" question. Of prime importance, he noted, is not the number of people kept alive, but the quality of their lives.

"This is a courageous age, but it has a different sense of values from the ages which have gone before," Lord Dawson said. "It looks upon life more from the point of view of quality than of quantity. It places less value on life when its usefulness has come to an end. There has gradually crept into medical opinion, as it has crept into lay opinion, the feeling that one should make the act of dying more gentle; and also more peaceful, even if it does involve the curtailment of the length of life."

In 1947 a voluntary euthanasia bill was placed before the General Assembly of the State of New York. The bill provided for the following:

1. Any sane person over twenty-one, suffering from painful and fatal disease, may petition a court of record for euthanasia, in a signed petition and attested document, with an affidavit from the attending physician that in his opinion the disease is incurable.
2. The court shall appoint a commission of three, of whom at least two shall be physicians, to investigate all aspects of the case and report back to the courts whether the patient understands the purpose of his petition and comes under the provisions of the act.
3. Upon a favorable report by the commission the court shall grant the petition and, if it is still wanted by the patient, euthanasia may be administered by a physician or any other person chosen by the patient or by the commission.

Although this proposal failed, there were many who were sympathetic to its principle. Ironically, many were opposed to the particular proposal because of the elaborate precautions it contained against abuse and misuse.

In 1968, the Euthanasia Society of England, after a thorough educational campaign designed to win support for legalized voluntary euthanasia, prepared a draft bill on the subject. The bill would have authorized physicians to give euthanasia to a patient "who is thought on reasonable grounds to be suffering from an irremediable physical condition of a distressing character, and who has, not less than thirty days previously, made a declaration requesting the administration of euthanasia in certain specified circumstances one or more of which has eventuated."

Lord Raglan, sponsor of the bill, argued that all persons should be allowed to die how and when they choose. Others argued that doctors should resist suggestions to end life. Others who were opposed to the proposal argued that

75

a good deal of unofficial movement toward euthanasia had already taken place and it was doubtful whether there was any necessity to enact laws when much understanding already existed. A respected surgeon, Lord Segal, admitted to the Lords that he had practiced both positive and negative euthanasia. Still, the House rejected the bill in 1969.

Persevering, the euthanasia forces in England continued their battle. In 1970 Dr. Hugh Gray of the Labor Party presented a bill in the House of Commons which would "make lawful administration of euthanasia at the request of the patient."

In the usually sedate House, Dr. Gray's bill was shouted down. In arguing for his measure he stated, "If I am involved in a motor accident on my way to the House and I suffer irreparable brain damage, I wish to be eased gently out of life. Call it suicide by proxy if you like—it is a choice which, as an adult, I should be able to make."

Florida legislator Walter Sackett, Jr., M.D. has proposed a "death with dignity" bill in his state's legislature every year since 1968. Initially his bill was presented as an amendment to the Basic Rights Article of the Florida State Constitution. "All natural persons are equal before the law and have inalienable rights, among which are the right to enjoy and defend life, liberty, *to be permitted to die with dignity,* to pursue happiness. . . . No person shall be deprived of any right because of race or religion."

The italicized words were his proposed addition. Recently, however, Dr. Sackett has changed his amendment to the form of a bill which, he says, represents a philosophy he has espoused throughout his medical life, "Death, like birth, is glorious—let it come easy."

The bill provides that a person can execute a document "directing that he shall have the right to death with dignity and his life shall not be prolonged beyond the point of a meaningful existence." The document would be drawn up requiring the same formalities as a last will and testament. Should an individual be unable to make such a decision himself because of mental or physical incapacity, the Sackett bill provides that it be made by his next of kin, or in their absence, by three physicians.

Neither the bill nor the amendment have passed, but Dr. Sackett continues his efforts. He recalls one of his most effective arguments: "I pointed out that any indecision in the closest of kin could be quickly resolved by posing the question: 'Now, that's you lying there, what do you want?' The response from hundreds has been, 'Oh, doctor, let me go.' At this point all hesitancy ceases and a clear-cut medical decision can follow."

There are a number of reasons why all of the euthanasia bills introduced in England and the United States thus far have failed to pass. Various objections have been voiced, ranging from those who have objected to disturbing the sick room with so many legal formalities, to those who feared the possible extension of the voluntary principle and the extension of permission to cover mentally defective children or the partially senile elderly. Opponents have also argued that some deaths are already almost certainly hastened by compassionate doctors with or without consent, tacit or otherwise, of the sufferers.

This is confirmed by many physicians who admit that passive euthanasia is frequently practiced in their hospitals. Others say that they know of physicians who have taken more active steps. One doctor recounts the action an older colleague takes when faced with a terminal patient in great pain. "He'll go to the patient and prescribe painkillers for him. He puts a bottle of the pills on the table next to the bed and tells the patient, 'Now, these pills are for your pain. *Take two every four hours: If you take them all they will kill you.'* "

British zoologist-anthropologist Dr. Desmond Morris believes that there are some areas where laws simply cannot be strictly enforced realistically. With regard to euthanasia he says, "There are certain laws where, under certain circumstances, you just don't push it if somebody breaks the rule because it would be impossible to really tidy up the law without giving too much power to some person. I think you have to keep the rule that no life can be taken, but make it a rule that is enforced with humanity and understanding."

This viewpoint has much-deserved support, but the question remains: Who will be empowered to enforce the laws with humanity and understanding? Will it be the courts, the family, the state, or the physician?

Lacking any crystal-clear criteria it is logical that physicians have already been appointed, if unofficially, to the task. After polling members of the Association of Professors of Medicine, Dr. R. H. Williams of the University of Washington reported that 87 per cent of those responding said they favored negative euthanasia. Fully 80 per cent said they themselves had practiced it. Only 15 per cent of the questionees voted in favor of positive euthanasia.

In a related study of staff physicians and first- and fourth-year medical students at a community hospital, researchers found that 59 per cent of the physicians, 69 per cent of the first-year students, and 90 per cent of the fourth-year students favored negative euthanasia. At the same time 27 per cent of the physicians, and 46 per cent of the first- and fourth-year medical students favored positive euthanasia.

Since law in our society isn't really an accurate reflection of the sentiments of the community and professions, it can be expected that as laymen and physicians become more willing to discuss actions that they already tacitly condone, laws will be changed. A similar process has taken place during recent years in the debate over abortion laws. The evolutionary process began in 1959 with the American Law Institute's model code recommendations, and continues today with heated discussion in state legislatures seeking to update their laws.

Reform in the laws governing those areas where moral opinion is involved is difficult. Politicians are aware that there are few votes to be gained through law reform, but there are many votes to be lost through offending sectarian groups. Legislators to even a greater degree than the general public are strongly affected by traditional mores, generalizations, and taboos. It is not easy to be in the forefront of a legal reform movement, especially, as is the case with euthanasia, when no country in the world has yet legalized voluntary euthanasia in the case of terminal illness and suffering.

Some countries have taken steps, however. Switzerland has laws that allow the physician to put a poison in the hand of the patient, but not actually administer it himself. In Norway a judge may reduce the punishment for mercy killing below the minimum penalty normally fixed by law.

England's Suicide Act of 1961 states that it is not illegal to attempt to commit suicide under any circumstances, although it is forbidden to assist another's suicide.

These beginnings are as far as any country has yet ventured toward legalizing any form of euthanasia. Some say that more countries have not taken such steps because of certain practical factors relating to the administration of existing laws against euthanasia. Law professor Glanville Williams notes that some of the same things that work against the passage of an actual law, work in favor of a nonwritten law permitting the practice.

First of all, Williams notes, because of the evidence required it is very difficult to establish a charge against a physician who "murders" through the administration of a humane overdose of drugs. When a patient has been receiving large doses of such a drug it is nearly impossible to determine the final dose, or even whether it actually caused the death. Secondly, prosecutors naturally will be reluctant to take action against a reputable physician who performed an act in good faith in a difficult situation. Third, juries will be reluctant to convict a physician under such circumstances. And finally, even if the worst occurs and the physician is convicted of murder, executive clemency will most likely intervene to prevent the death penalty.

Even with the lack of statute or case law to support voluntary euthanasia, England's Euthanasia Society, as well as its American sister organization, have produced documents designed to aid those wishing euthanasia for themselves. The American version is reproduced below:

TO MY FAMILY, MY PHYSICIAN,
MY CLERGYMAN, MY LAWYER

If the time comes when I can no longer take part in decisions for my own future, let this statement stand as the testament of my wishes:

I, _____ request that I be allowed to die and not be kept alive by artificial means or heroic measures. Death is as much a reality as birth, growth, maturity and old age—it is the one certainty. I do not fear death as much as I fear the indignity of deterioration, dependence and hopeless pain. I ask that drugs be mercifully administered to me for terminal suffering even if they hasten the moment of death.

This request is made after careful consideration. Although this document is not legally binding, you who care for me will, I hope, feel morally bound to follow its mandate. I recognize that it places a heavy burden of responsibility upon you, and it is with the intention of sharing that responsibility and of mitigating any feelings of guilt that this statement is made.

More than sixty thousand such documents have been distributed by America's Euthanasia Educational Fund. In spite of the fact that they are not legally binding, there are indications that increasing numbers of physicians are honoring the spirit of the documents. These physicians apparently hold that Glanville Williams is correct in his assumption that practical factors work against any conviction in lawsuits involving euthanasia.

In fact, the physician simply cannot avoid making the judgment as to whether or not a life should be maintained. In essence, the doctor makes a decision about euthanasia each time he has to order a life-sustaining medication for a fatally ill patient. When several treatments are available, such as surgery, chemicals, or radiotherapy, the doctor has to decide which treatment will be performed, if any. He has to decide whether one treatment that provides less physical and mental stress, but possibly a shortened life, may be better than one that prolongs the life to a greater degree, but with greater suffering.

Indeed, there is no place for the physician to find absolutes. Certainly he cannot seek them among philosophers or theologians, for they have no more resolved the dilemma. As is normal in such serious moral matters, major religions are split, even within themselves, on the issue. The physician seeking support for his belief in "death with dignity" can, however, find it even among the most orthodox, for there are interpretations of religious doctrines that offer a wide scope for such beliefs.

In a 1961 article in the *Hebrew Medical Journal,* Rabbi Immanuel Jakobovits says that "any form of active euthanasia is strictly prohibited and condemned as plain murder. . . . Anyone who kills a dying person is liable to the death penalty as a common murderer. At the same time, Jewish law sanctions the withdrawal of any factor—whether extraneous to the patient himself or not—which may artificially delay his demise in the final phase."

The rabbi points out, however, that according to rabbinical references, this refers to an individual who is expected to die within three days or less. In other words, passive euthanasia in a patient who may live for weeks or months may not be condoned. Without doubt, some Jewish authorities would take a stricter view. On the other hand, Jews of the Conservative and Reform traditions are likely to be far more liberal.

The Roman Catholic view as espoused by Pope Pius XII is better known. If life is ebbing hopelessly, the pope said, doctors may cease their efforts, thus "to permit the patient, already virtually dead, to pass on in peace." He noted that heroic measures are not indicated in hopeless situations. Going a step further, the pope said that treatment with painkillers is permissible when the relieving of unbearable pain is achieved by the use of drugs that will shorten life, "provided that no other means exist, and if, in the given circumstances, that action does not prevent the carrying out of other moral and religious duties." The pope made it clear, however, that positive euthanasia without the patient's consent was murder; and with his consent, suicide. "What is morally a crime cannot, under any pretext, become legal," the pontiff declared.

A few years ago the Most Rev. Fulton J. Sheen, auxiliary bishop of New York, said, "If the doctor told me that extraordinary means would be needed and I was lying with a body full of tubes to keep me alive, I would ask him to take them out. There is no moral difficulty at such a situation." Rev. Sheen made the statement at a news conference in Atlantic City with Dr. Edward Rynearson of the Mayo Clinic. Dr. Rynearson, a Methodist who has often spoken out against the practice of prolonging life after medical hope is gone, said that it was "wrong for doctors to see how long we can keep 'vegetables' alive. . . . With enough tubes in a person and surrounded by oxygen, there is hardly any way he can die."

Bishop Sheen made it clear that, if a family desired it,

the physician should continue life-prolonging treatment, but added that if Dr. Rynearson "was the doctor, I'd take his advice."

In the Protestant Church it has been said that there are "all possible colors in the spectrum of attitudes toward euthanasia." It is true, however, that Protestants in general tend to be more liberal, and many advocate judging each case individually.

The very fact that all of this discussion of euthanasia has been made necessary speaks poorly of our society. As Dr. John Hinton has concluded in his book *Dying,* "It seems a terrible indictment that the main argument for euthanasia is that many suffer unduly because there is a lack of preparation and provision for the total care of the dying."

> "Nothing in life is to be feared.
> It is to be understood."
> *Marie Curie*

4

THE DYING
PATIENT

Brian P. was fifty, but looked younger. He was recovering from an operation in which part of his stomach was removed because of cancer. Afterward the man had been hopeful and looked forward to his retirement in a few years. Instead of improving, however, Mr. P. lost weight and grew increasingly weak. He became more and more depressed at the thought of his demise.

The man's wife continually assured him that nothing was wrong and that he would soon regain his former health and vigor. Still the man's condition worsened and soon forced him to enter the hospital again. This time malignant tumors were discovered in his lungs. Nevertheless his wife seemed to remain convinced he would recover, and during visits to the hospital she continually reminded him of his promise to buy a "retirement" home in the Southwest.

When the couple's daughter came home from college for a visit with her father she was visibly shocked to see his condition. "You have to get well," she told him. After the daughter departed, her father thought regretfully about her childhood and all the time he had spent away from his family involved in his business. He had limited his time at work after his first operation, but by that time his daughter had already gone away to school.

Although Mr. P.'s recovery was doubtful, and he was always in great pain, his family continually reminded him how much he was needed and how they expected a rapid improvement in his health. The nurses encouraged him to eat more, and his doctors kept talking to him about the possibility of another operation. Somewhat justifiably Mr. P. felt that there was nobody with whom he could talk about the seriousness of his condition.

One afternoon a hospital psychiatrist visited him and said that she would be available if he wanted to talk about anything. The patient spoke in a soft, weak voice and told her that each of his waking moments was agony because he had failed to fulfill his family's expectation. "I want to sleep, sleep, sleep and not wake up. How can a man die in peace when everyone wants him to get well?" he asked.

The psychiatrist then intervened with the family in an attempt to help them help the patient die more comfortably. She explained that the man was facing his impending death courageously, but their refusal to "let him go" was making it infinitely more difficult. The patient was ready to separate himself from this world, the psychiatrist said, so ordering additional medical treatment would only prevent him from finding the relief he sought in sleep.

Mr. P. apparently suffered much more from the feeling that he had disappointed his family than he did from the pain and physical discomfort of his disease. Once his relatives were able to accept the reality of the situation, they stopped trying to urge him back to health and the man was able to die in peace.

Daily in the United States some five thousand persons die. Some die easily; more do not. Some die suddenly of trauma and others die lingering deaths. But of vital importance is that many of them die with a great deal of mental anguish because they or their relatives did not know what to expect or how to react to each other. How many individuals must suffer agonies similar to Brian P.'s because there were no willing or available family members, nurses, or physicians who would discuss the real situation with them? Death, like birth, is natural. It is a part of life that cannot be escaped. Nevertheless, more often than not, we avoid going to the aid of family and friends and helping them through life's final experience in an understanding way. One reason this is true, perhaps, is that by doing so individuals are forcefully reminded of the inevitability of their own death.

"Our embarrassment at the individual face of death," says Dr. Herman Feifel, professor of psychiatry at the University of Southern California, "forces the seriously ill and dying person to live alone on the brink of an abyss with no one to understand him."

Indeed, while modern medicine has done a great deal to help overcome physical pain, it has accomplished precious little in the way of easing the final burden of loneliness. The dying must face the possibilities of emotional pain, grief, and indignity—and they must face them alone. Today's society has failed to provide a model, an ideal to be striven for in dying.

"The sting of death is solitude," says theologian Paul Ramsey in *Patient as Person*. "Desertion is more choking than death and more feared."

Death is simply un-American. Its inevitability is an affront to our inalienable rights of "life, liberty, and the pursuit of happiness." In *Man's Concern with Death,* historian Arnold Toynbee sees even broader implications in the American approach to death. "If the fact of death were once admitted to be a reality even in the United States, then it would also have to be admitted that the United States is not the earthly paradise that it is deemed to be."

But dying, natural process that it is for mortal men, need not be so difficult. "If you see anyone distressed at the prospect of dying," remarked Socrates in the *Phaedo,* "it will be proof enough that he is a lover not of wisdom but of the body. As a matter of fact, I suppose he is also a lover of wealth and reputation."

Socrates himself spent the final day of his life in prison discussing his philosophy of life with his students and friends. Even while he drank the fatal cup of hemlock the courageous philosopher maintained tranquility of body and mind. In his final words he asked that thanks be given for him to the God of Healing, for in his death this great man saw the cure for life.

In fact the dying have often been known to show great compassion for the living who attend them. At age twenty-eight the poet John Keats was dying of tuberculosis. His friend Severn was at the bedside and Keats asked him, "Severn, have you ever seen anyone die?" The answer was "No," and Keats became apologetic. "I don't think I'll be convulsed and it won't last for very long."

Then Severn observed an unearthly brightness in the poet's eyes and the phlegm rose up in the dying man's throat. "Severn, lift me up, I am dying. I shall die easy. Don't be frightened. Thank God it has come." John Keats died so quietly that his friend thought he had fallen asleep.

But even when the threat of death lingers, an individual can make valuable use of his remaining days. "It is encouraging to note," says psychiatrist Feifel, "that the threat of death can function as an integrative, rather than disruptive event for certain individuals. One can learn, apparently, not only to adjust to inordinate stress, but to grow and change under its spur."

After a twenty-nine-year-old mother of two boys learned of her fatal illness she said, "I was always worried about the bills and making ends meet. After the doctor told me I had cancer, I stopped and took a hard look around. I never realized how wonderful simply being alive could be. I don't think this new feeling will make my end more difficult. At least I was really alive for a few months."

The famous psychologist Abraham Maslow made similar observations shortly before his death in 1970. Recalling his feelings after a previous heart attack, he wrote of the satisfaction he felt in just having completed what he considered his most important work. "I had really spent myself. This was the best I could do and here was a good time to die. . . . It was like a good ending [in a play]." After his heart attack Maslow referred to his "post mortem life" which he keenly enjoyed. "If you're reconciled with death or even if you are pretty well assured that you will have a good death, a dignified one, then every single day is transformed because the pervasive undercurrent—the fear of death—is removed."

Most men do not so readily accept death or obviate their fear of it. Perhaps, however, it is the fear of death and dying that is exaggerated. A 1970 study of 183 middle-aged to elderly persons at the University of Southern California found that 63 per cent of the sample said they were not afraid to die. The men and women ranged in age from fifty to eighty-six and were generally found to be well adjusted and not preoccupied with death or dying. Furthermore, in addition to the 63 per cent who said they were not worried at the prospect of death, another 28 per cent described themselves as "not very fearful," while the rest, only 9 per cent, were "fairly fearful."

Traditionally we have presumed that most aging persons are fearful, apprehensive, and preoccupied with death and dying. The USC study, however, seems clearly to have refuted this idea. Along the same lines it has been found that younger individuals are equally unafraid of their own deaths—or at least say they are. Recent, but informal studies have mirrored a classic 1935 study of college students at DePauw and Butler universities in which Warren C. Middleton found that only about 12 per cent of the subjects had a strong fear or horror of death, 25 per cent were absolutely unafraid, and 62 per cent said their attitude toward death was one of indifference. An overwhelming majority of these students (93 per cent) said that they thought of their own deaths very rarely and only 8 per cent imagined that death would be painful. Studies indicate, in fact, that this majority is correct in their assumption.

In the late 1880s, renowned clinician and teacher Sir William Osler reported on a series of five hundred deathbed cases in which he studied the modes of death and sensations accompanying the process. Of the five hundred, only 18 per cent suffered bodily pain and only 2 per cent suffered mental apprehension as death grew very near. Sir William concluded: "We speak of death as the king of terrors and yet how rarely the act of dying appears to be painful. How rarely do we witness agony in the last hours. Strict, indeed, is the fell sergeant in his arrest but few feel the iron grip. The hard process of nature's law is for most of us mercifully affected, and death, like birth, is but a sleep and a forgetting."

Data to the contrary notwithstanding, however, it is clear that facing up to death and dying (or to real or imagined pain or mental anguish) is something to be feared.

Dr. Robert Kastenbaum, a psychologist and director of Wayne State University's Center for Psychological Studies of Dying, Death, and Lethal Behavior, cites a study that supports the contention that there is barely any relationship between what people think that they think about death and the way they actually feel about it when it must be faced. If correct, this theory would render practically useless most of the "fear of death" surveys discussed earlier in this chapter.

Kastenbaum's researchers interviewed a group of housewives whose stated attitudes toward death ranged from strong faith in personal immortality to stoic acceptance. The women were then invited to visit a number of hospital patients. They were told that some of the patients were terminal cases and others were simply sick. Regardless of how the women said they viewed death, they all had a tendency to move close and talk animatedly with the "merely sick," while they inched away from those they thought were dying and looked anywhere but at these patients.

Such apparent confusion among the living puts the dying in quite a predicament. They "no longer know what role to play. Most of them are already old and therefore 'worthless' by our standards. There's simply no place for a human death when the dying person is regarded as a machine coming to a stop," Kastenbaum says.

Many professionals believe that one reason we cannot easily cope with death, or the fear of it, is that we rarely witness a single death in our early lives. Current longevity coupled with increased family mobility, has severely limited man's perception of death. Most Americans, too, expect to die away from home, and all but about one-third will die in hospitals or in old-age homes, called "human junkyards" by some. Meanwhile, their grandchildren can expect to grow to maturity without ever witnessing the death of a loved one.

As philosopher Lewis Mumford observed at age seventy-four, "The generations need each other. When death was a family affair, it brought the generations together. Now, it seems, death keeps the generations apart."

Indeed death may be profoundly significant for the individual experiencing it as well as his family. It is a climax, the end of a relationship, the last stage of life. A dying man may view his life in perspective and increase his maturity or strengthen his faith. As psychiatrist Russell Noyes, of the University of Iowa, observes, "The person who maintains his dignity and courage while dying in effect preserves it for a lifetime and for the memory of his surviving family."

According to Dr. Noyes we fear most three aspects of the prospect of our own death. First, we fear the unfamiliar ideas that surround death today. Fear of the ending of life itself is the second aspect of death-caused fear. The dying person fears the end to wealth and status, the end to family relationships, and the end of striving toward still unrealized goals. When the living grieve, they usually are faced only with the loss of a single friend or family member, but the dying individual must grieve the loss of all friends and relatives as well as himself.

The final aspect of death which contributes to fear concerns the afterlife. Death has always been thought to be a type of punishment; is it not natural to fear punishment, especially when it is an unknown?

These fears are often intensified in the patient who is unsure of the true status of his health. One middle-aged woman, a victim of cancer, complained to her physician that she felt nervous; she had lost some sixty pounds, her priest kept visiting her, and her mother-in-law had never been so pleasant, even though the woman admitted "I've never been meaner to her."

"You mean you think you're dying?" the physician asked.

"I do," the woman answered.

When the physician told her she was right, she broke into a smile and said, "Well, I've finally broken the silence barrier. Someone has finally told me the truth."

The woman was one of sixteen incurable cancer patients, in the Boston area, whose reactions were studied over a five-year period in the late 1950s and early 1960s by two Harvard psychiatrists, Thomas Hackett and Avery

Weisman. The result of the study was the contention that dying patients should be told the truth, even if only to relieve them of the terrible duty of pretending to be optimistic about their chances when they expect the worse.

The physicians found that the patients they studied all had some suspicion of their impending death, even though they had not been told of it. All patients were relieved to have their suspicions confirmed. Hackett and Weisman concluded that even if the truth encourages the dying person to let go of his hold on life, the telling is proper. When the scientists presented their findings from this study to the 1961 meeting of the American Psychiatric Association, many of their colleagues disagreed. Argued Dr. Charles W. Wahl, "Never deprive a patient of hope. The torture of capital punishment is not death, but knowing exactly when death will occur." A dozen years later the same controversy is still reflected in seminars and articles in professional journals. A more detailed discussion of the question of whether or not to tell a dying patient his prognosis can be found in the chapter "Doctors and Death."

Though disagreement exists in this area, physicians generally feel that each case must be recognized as unique and warrants careful consideration on its own merits. The study of the act of dying and its effects on the patient and family is a new field. With man's tendency to reject the dying, and his tendency to avoid or exaggerate his own fears concerning the future, the question may rightly be asked: How are we to learn more about the dying?

A similar question was asked several years ago of Swiss-born psychiatrist Dr. Elisabeth Kübler-Ross by four theology students who were writing a paper about behavior in time of crisis. Death, they agreed, was the greatest crisis imaginable. Dr. Ross, a member of the University of Chicago Hospital staff, decided to interview those who knew most about the experience, the dying themselves. "When I wanted to know what it was like to be schizophrenic," she told the theology students, "I spent a lot of time with schizophrenics. Why not do the same thing with dying patients? We will sit together and ask them to be our teachers."

To her surprise, Dr. Ross found that she encountered stubborn resistance from physicians. "Suddenly there wasn't a dying patient in the hospital." Since those days of initial resistance, however, Dr. Ross has broken through the "silence barrier" and, with colleagues, has interviewed more than five hundred dying patients and their families. She found that the patients themselves were more than willing, even anxious, to discuss their fears and concerns. Many obtained great relief from the seminars and were very appreciative that someone was willing to listen. In fact, only three of one group of more than two hundred subjects refused an invitation to speak to one of the seminars, which were conducted behind a one-way window while doctors, nurses, clergymen, and other observers watched and listened.

After many months of seminars and interviews Dr. Ross concluded that most terminally ill persons experience a series of five stages in their anticipation of death.

The first stage is denial, when the patient refuses to admit the seriousness of his illness. During this stage the patient often visits several different physicians searching for one who will make a different diagnosis, asking for new drugs, new tests, or yet another consultation. In short, the patient searches for affirmation of the fact that he was right in saying at the outset, "This can't be happening to me."

Dr. Ross tells the story of a man in her hospital, a rich, important, and powerful man, whose wife came to the psychiatrist because her husband had been treating her so badly. The psychiatrist went to visit him. "I walked in and right away he was saying, 'I didn't ask to see you, did I? All that's wrong with me is malnutrition.' Now what was that man saying? What does it mean for a millionaire to say he's got malnutrition? He had leukemia, but malnutrition is something he could control. He couldn't accept being sick because he had to feel that he was in charge of his situation."

It is well accepted, however, that there are some patients who need denial, and this should be respected. One woman, for example, said that she had been a fighter all her life and she wanted to keep on fighting right up to the end.

For the millionaire with leukemia, though, the hospital staff cooperated in devising a treatment plan. Instead of simply giving the man a back rub at a specific time, the nurse would ask him when it would be most convenient. His wife followed the same pattern by calling to ask when she should visit and whether she should bring the children. This routine gave the patient some control over what was happening to him in the hospital and it enabled him to acknowledge his illness and cope with it.

When a patient lets go of denial as a defense he often enters a stage of profound anger, a why-should-this-happen-to-me attitude. One man, for example, was extremely resentful that his serious illness could not have happened to someone else, perhaps the local drunk and trouble maker in his home town. In the stage of anger a patient may lash out at doctors, nurses, family, or friends. Such offensive behavior in the patient is understandable, though it may be trying. The patient is attempting to marshal all of his life forces. He is reacting to the life and energy of others—for these are the very things he is in the process of losing.

The psychiatrist advises those in contact with patients in this second stage to encourage them to express their anger. A desire to scream or cry or verbalize resentment is normal and patients who do release their emotions can often find relief.

Resentment gives way to the third stage of the process of dying, a period of bargaining. This stage is more subtle than the others, and more private. The difficult patient may suddenly become cooperative, and the reward he seeks for this good behavior is a stay of execution—a few more days or weeks to live. Often the patient, like a small child, tries to make a deal with God for more time and less suffering. One does not usually observe patients in this stage because the bargaining is often carried out late at night in their prayers, wishes, and dreams.

In a more open instance of bargaining an opera singer, victim of a fatal skin cancer, begged for a chance to perform one last time, thus death would have to wait. She did, and it did.

Another woman who had been in the hospital for a long time, in acute pain from a terminal disease, wanted more than anything else to have one painless day away from the hospital so she could attend her son's wedding. "We arranged permission," Dr. Ross recalls, "and she went out looking radiantly beautiful." When, after the wedding, the woman returned to the hospital, she immediately told her doctor, "Don't forget, I have another son."

Such bargaining is nothing new. In 1109, when St. Anselm, Archbishop of Canterbury, lay dying, he told fellow clerics gathered at his deathbed: "I shall gladly obey His call. Yet I should also feel grateful if He would grant me a little longer time with you, and if I could be permitted to solve a question—the origin of the soul." The wish was not granted, but even if it had been, another bargain probably would have been quickly proposed.

There is some evidence to indicate that the bargaining stage may indeed be fruitful physically as well as psychologically. David P. Phillips of the State University of New York, at Stony Brook, contends that dying must certainly be a form of social behavior. In several studies the sociologist has found that people who are about to die seem to hold onto life until after a birthday, an election, a religious holiday, or another event to which they look forward.

In a survey of the death dates of more than one thousand two hundred famous Americans listed in *Four Hundred Notable Americans* and *Who Was Who,* Phillips found that they died least often in the months before their birthdays and most frequently in the three months following them. Phillips believes that this may hold true especially for famous persons because they have more to look forward to in a birthday celebration.

There is much anecdotal material that substantiates this theory of the vital buoyancy of optimism. Both Thomas Jefferson and John Adams, for example, died on July 4, fifty years after the signing of the Declaration of Independence. No coincidence, says Phillips, who notes that Jefferson's last words, as quoted by his physician, were, "About seven o'clock of the evening of that day, [Jefferson] awoke, and seeing me standing at his bedside exlaimed, 'Oh, Doctor, are you still there?' in a voice, however, that was husky and indistinct. He then asked, 'Is it the Fourth?' to which I replied, 'It soon will be.' These were the last words I heard him utter."

Phillips has also discovered that between 1875 and 1915 the death rate in Budapest, which had a large Jewish population, declined markedly during the month before Yom Kippur, day of atonement. This pre-Yom Kippur "death dip" also occurred between 1921 and 1965 in New York City, which also has a large Jewish population. And in the dramatic weeks before every United States election between 1904 and 1964, the nationwide death rate showed a marked decline.

After denial, anger, and bargaining, the dying person will become deeply depressed in a period of preparatory grief. The person mourns for what he has already suffered and grieves the loss of everything and everyone he loves. As a person in this stage contemplates death, he often will turn away and cry privately. Sometimes staff members or relatives will react to this behavior by being overly cheerful, making statements such as, "Come on now, things aren't so bad."

"Not so bad for whom?" Dr. Ross asks. "Why should he be cheerful? Simply because those around him are uncomfortable by his appropriate sadness?"

This period of grief is very important. "He may not want to see his family—they may remind him of the magnitude of his impending loss. And the family may feel rejected, as if the patient doesn't love them anymore. But he must be allowed to disassociate himself from life before he's ready to accept death with peace and dignity."

With the proper reassurance and preparation the patient next reaches the fifth and final stage, acceptance. "I think this is the miracle," one patient said. "I am ready now and not even afraid anymore," she said shortly before her death. The stage of acceptance is a courageous time when a person has accepted the reality of mortality. It marks victory over resignation. Instead of giving up, the patient recounts his life and severs his relationships with the knowledge that the end will bring relief.

However, the family must be careful not to intrude upon the patient too greatly during this last stage. One woman, after her dying husband reached the stage of acceptance, invited all the relatives to the hospital to visit. The woman wanted her husband to play the part of the entertaining host as he had always done at home. In her attempt to maintain a semblance of normality, she could not see beyond her own needs and burdened him with responsibility as he was seeking solitude.

Psychiatrists generally agree that the dying need not go through the various stages exactly as outlined here. Rather a person can move back and forth between stages, or even not experience a certain stage. Some religious persons may reach the stage of acceptance long before illness and death are realities.

During the process of dying, however, the most important consideration is to focus on the individual patient's needs, both physically and emotionally. Those in attendance must be ready to anticipate and fulfill the patients' requests, so far as they are able, instead of selfishly imposing their will upon them.

To help concentrate more on the needs of the dying, and make the final months easier, special homes, called hospices, have been designed, and a few have already been built. The word *hospice* actually means "a place where travelers are given rest and hospitality and where a home is made for those who are in need or sickness." Proponents of the hospice concept believe that hospitals are not optimum locations for terminally ill patients. The pace and purpose of the general hospital centers around restoring patients to health and discharging them from the hospital as soon as possible. The dying often are relegated to a room at the end of the hall, which nurses tend to avoid and physicians find time to visit only after they have finished their rounds.

Observes Dr. Melvin Krant, associate professor of medicine at Tufts University Medical School, "Citadel of medical progress, the hospital ironically becomes a center of frustration and conflict when confronted with the dying patient. On one hand, most Americans, separated from death most of their lives, call on the hospital for professional skills to help the dying patient. On the other, the mainstream of work of the hospital, which places greatest value on cure or rehabilitation, leads away from the dying patient."

While nursing and old-age homes may perform a certain function, they often lack full-time medical personnel, or nurses and aides adequately trained in talking to and caring for the dying. Routines are rigid and too often the emphasis is more on getting the patient away from a home situation, where he has been a burden, to surroundings where he will be "cared for." Unfortunately this care in nursing homes is all too often unrewarding, cold, and impersonal.

Life in the hospice, on the other hand, is flexible enough to accommodate to the wishes of the patient, who does what he wants and is able to do. The patient is active in decisions concerning himself as long as is possible. He is, as he should be, a key member of the treatment team composed not only of doctors, nurses, and clergymen, but the patient's family as well.

The oldest hospice is St. Joseph's in London. This facility, with a total of 150 beds, is a religious foundation established in 1902 by the Irish Sisters of Charity, a Roman Catholic order of nuns. It welcomes all, however, without distinction as to race or creed. Even though most of the nursing staff are Roman Catholics, the majority of patients are not.

Of the 150 beds, 40 or 50 are kept for patients with terminal, malignant diseases with a prognosis of three months or less to live. Patients are referred by other hospitals or their doctors. Only about 10 per cent live longer than expected. The rest of the beds in St. Joseph's are for the frail with no place else to go and for patients with lingering illnesses who are not suited for the normal hospital. None of the patients in St. Joseph's are candidates for rehabilitation.

Today the leader of the hospice movement is Dr. Cicely Saunders, who for six years held a clinical research fellowship working at St. Joseph's. Originally trained as a nurse and medical social worker, Dr. Saunders has also become a physician. In 1967 she opened another, smaller hospice, St. Christopher's of London. Much of Dr. Saunders's early planning for St. Christopher's took place in the years she served at St. Joseph's.

St. Christopher's cost about $15 million, all of which was contributed. The first gift came from a young patient who died and left £500 to Dr. Saunders. Dr. Saunders recalls the patient saying, "I only want what is in your mind and in your heart." The same sentiment was echoed years later by another patient who told the physician, "Thank you. And not just for the pills but for your heart."

"I think both of them showed that they wanted not only skill but compassion also," Dr. Saunders says. "They needed warmth and friendship as well as good technical care."

The hospice, she explains, "does not have the challenge of diagnosis nor the difficult decision concerning treatment. Others have wrestled with these problems for our patients; those stages of their illness are now over.

"We do not have the hope of cure, but it is easier for us to look at our patients as persons in distress and to concentrate on giving them relief."

At St. Christopher's patients are admitted because they are dying, usually of cancer. But this is no "home for incurables" in the old sense of the phrase. Photographs and sketches of patients invariably show them looking comfortable and content, playing cards, or sitting in the garden. Visitors always comment on their relaxed and smiling faces. There is a children's playground in the hospice yard, and here the children of staff members play. The youngsters are looked after while their parents are working and they join them for lunch in the dining room. At play on the grounds the children give pleasure and diversion to the patient-residents, who often join them in the yard. The atmosphere at St. Christopher's has been designed to create an environment in which these patients can be cared for with love and understanding.

"I believe that to talk of accepting death when its approach is inevitable is not mere resignation or submission on the part of the patient, nor defeat or neglect on the part of the doctor; for each of them accepting death's coming is the very opposite of doing nothing," Dr. Saunders has written.

Another aspect of the hospice concept is a home-care program to enable future patients to meet staff members, who in turn can acquaint them with the hospice facilities. The residents and staff of St. Christopher's consider themselves to be a "family" in the very real sense of the word. The hospice is a place to die, but a place at which the patient can receive the kind of care he needs in his final days, care that the family is not able to give at home. Still, the family plays an important role at the hospice. Visiting hours are open, youthful visitors are encouraged, and rooms are designed to accommodate a number of family members instead of just one or two visitors.

One patient, spending Christmas at St. Christopher's surrounded by her family, said, "I am perfectly content to be here and have experienced such peace that, at times, it is quite overwhelming; I have never known anything like it in my life before. . . . I was to spend Christmas at home, but was not well enough to go. I was happy to stay here. . . .

"I cannot really explain what it is that is so different here," the woman continued, "nor why I have experienced such peace. When I was in the other hospital there were twenty-eight of us in the ward and so many people died that I found it upsetting and depressing. When I returned home I could still hear the sound of the trolley which used to take away the patients who died."

The dying patients at St. Christopher's are invariably so quiet and peaceful that they are not moved away from their four- or six-person rooms when death is imminent, but remain there until they die.

"We are trying to make dying more human and meaningful," says Florence S. Wald, vice president of Hospice, Inc., a group of clergymen, laymen, and medical professionals in the New Haven, Connecticut, area who are trying to raise $3 million to build America's first hospice. The projected facility would initially provide beds for seventy patients and room for out-patient care for seventy more.

The cost to patients would average 69 per cent of that of a general hospital, according to the Rev. Edward Dobihal, director of Religious Ministries at Yale New Haven Hospital and president of Hospice, Inc.

One principle of the New Haven hospice, already in effect at the British institutions, would be that none of the "heroic measures" would be used to prolong the life of a terminal patient—no antibiotics, no radiation therapy, no resuscitators, or cardiac massage. The most important medications given to hospice patients are painkillers. These are to relieve the patient of as much physical pain as possible while, at the same time, helping him to remain alert. Patients, in fact, do not like being doped up and if given their choice of total pain control or some discomfort they tend to endure the discomfort in order to remain alert. "Our aim," says Dr. Saunders, "should be full relief combined with a capacity to enjoy friends and food and all of the activity that is possible."

Physicians and allied personnel are currently taking part in serious discussions over the use of various narcotic drugs for the dying patient. Such treatment is not intended for the comatose, but for those who, in their final days or weeks, are suffering unbearable pain. For years physicians have administered morphine to dull severe pain, but in the British hospices physicians such as Dr. Saunders have found that heroin—illegal under any circumstances in the United States, but not in Britain—is a preferable narcotic for terminal cancer patients.

Dr. R. G. Twycross, a St. Christopher's staff member, explains that patients are given a mixture of sugar water laced with heroin, alcohol, cocaine, and a tranquilizer. The dosage for each patient is designed to keep him free of pain until his next dose. Medical personnel do not wait for patients to develop pain and request medication, but give it to them prophylactically. And in such a situation, physicians have found that patients rarely develop an addiction to the drug. "Patients do not develop a craving for the drug when they no longer have to crave relief for their pain," Dr. Twycross says. Heroin has helped some patients to stop vomiting, regain their appetite, improve in mood, and become more cooperative with staff in their last days.

In their desire to help comfort the dying, physicians also have begun to search for new ways of alleviating pain without affecting—in fact enhancing, if possible—the patient's psyche. Some have turned to hypnosis, or self-hypnosis, and recently two scientists speculated on the possibility of using acupuncture to alleviate terminal suffering.

"In view of the apparently successful relief of operative pain by acupuncture, it seems logical to seek to relieve pain in the terminal patient similarly. If drug-induced stupor could be replaced by analgesia achieved by acupuncture, the implications to the care of the terminal patient are obvious," report Dr. Austin Kutscher and Dr. Lester Mark, of Columbia University.

Other scientists continue all-out search for an effective pharmacopoeia. One group of Baltimore physicians, led by Dr. Stanislav Grof, has begun studying the effects of psychedelic drugs on the mental and physical states of patients with terminal cancer. The work, at Maryland's Psychiatric Research Center, is in its early stages, but physicians are finding that the psychedelics—LSD or a similar drug called DPT—are often of great help to the dying. The following case history illustrates in brief the Maryland Center's method of LSD treatment and its effect on one patient.

Mrs. Davis (a pseudonym), a fifty-eight-year-old woman, had suffered from breast cancer for twelve years. In spite of a number of surgical and medical procedures the disease had spread to her spine. When the woman was first referred for LSD treatment, pressure on her spinal nerves had caused numbness and paralysis of the lower half of her body. At the first interview, the patient was anxious and depressed.

After a week of preparatory psychotherapy with the patient and her family, the nature and purpose of the treatment were explained. The day before the LSD session, flowers were brought into Mrs. Davis's room and a portable stereo record player was set up.

On the day of the treatment, the patient was given LSD. Classical music was played in her room to help with relaxation and expression. A physician and trained nurse were present during the entire session (as they are in every similar session with other patients). The first few hours of the session went well and at one point Mrs. Davis exclaimed, "This is one of the happiest days of my life. I will always remember it." The short episodes of apprehension, confusion, and paranoia that did occur were easily handled by reassurance and support by the medical personnel.

During the session Mrs. Davis took part in a realistic discussion as to whether she would ever walk again. She was reluctant to accept the idea that if she were confined to bed her life could go on. "However, the patient spontaneously expressed her determination to try her best in physiotherapy, in spite of the odds against her. She was supported in her decision to try, but also discussed was acceptance of her condition, if it could not be improved," a physician noted.

Later the same day Mrs. Davis came out of her "trance" and her family visited. It was a time of closeness and sharing and the family commented on the change in her mental outlook from "anxiety and depression to one of peace and joy."

Six days after the LSD session the patient, cheerful and hopeful, went home where she worked with a physiotherapist and made unexpected progress. After six months she was doing a limited amount of walking with a cane.

In spite of accomplishments, Mrs. Davis retained feelings that she would remain an invalid, and became difficult to manage at home. The back brace worn out of bed was cumbersome and caused her to become increasingly depressed. At this time both the patient and family requested another LSD session.

Ten months after her initial LSD treatment, after being seen regularly in preparation, Mrs. Davis was readmitted to the hospital for another session. During the LSD treatment,

> She remembered patients she had known with cancer, and her fear of decaying flesh was symbolized by visions of vultures feeding on rotten meat. After confronting rather than retreating from these unpleasant feelings and experiences, the patient had the experience of passing through a series of blue curtains or veils. On the other side she felt as if she were a bird in a small cabin alone with the snow falling. She experienced wonderful feelings of peace and harmony and visions of beautiful colors like the rainbow. After this, the experience stabilized, and she had an enjoyable reliving of happy memories from her past.

Later, when Mrs. Davis's family arrived, she had a serene smile on her face, but would not elaborate on her experience. "You wouldn't believe me if I did tell you," she said.

Again Mrs. Davis left the hospital in good spirits and

participated in her daughter's wedding, walking down the aisle without a cane and amazing friends at the reception by dancing with her husband. "Her sister said she had been the life of the party."

Within six months, however, Mrs. Davis requested a third LSD session. She was suffering more pain. She had become discouraged because she had not worked for more than two years even though she still harbored hopes that she would someday return to her former job.

The session began smoothly, but the patient became frightened when she saw a huge wall of flames. After support and encouragement by the therapist, the patient was able to go through the middle of the flames, and at this point experienced positive ego transcendence. She felt that she had left her body, was in another world, and was in the presence of God who seemed symbolized by a huge diamond-shaped iridescent Presence. She did not see Him as a person, but knew He was there. The feeling was one of awe and reverence, and she was filled with a sense of peace and joy. When her family had arrived, she radiated a psychedelic afterglow of peace and beauty which all remarked upon.

That evening Mrs. Davis talked to her daughters about what might lie ahead. Soon she was discharged from the hospital in good spirits. One apparent effect of the LSD treatment was that when she suffered pain she could force it out of her mind by recalling her out-of-body LSD experience.

Mrs. Davis did well for about a month, until she slipped on some stairs and hurt her back. She then contracted flu and was confined to bed. These physical setbacks, and recurrence of severe pain, caused depression. A fourth session of LSD treatment was requested and almost six months after the third session the patient was readmitted.

During the final preparation for the session Mrs. Davis began asking direct questions about her diagnosis. This was the first time in nearly two years in the LSD-treatment program that she had done this, for, although she knew her breast had been removed because of a tumor, she thought there was no further growth. With the ever-increasing pain in her back, however, she began to wonder.

Her questions were answered gently, but without evasion, and the meaning and emotional impact were discussed with her. The family members were informed of this conversation immediately thereafter, and they reacted by becoming quite upset and angry. That very evening, in a general family discussion with the patient and therapist, however, most of them were able to resolve their feelings. Some felt embarrassed because of their previous pretense; most felt relieved when they saw how well the patient had dealt with the situation. The patient stated that she was glad to know the truth; she was obviously not psychologically shattered or further depressed as some of the family members had feared.

The next day, the LSD session went smoothly. Later in the evening the patient felt very close to her family and talked with each of them alone. Even though Mrs. Davis felt tired, she was reluctant to leave her family at the end of the day. In spite of her new knowledge, during the following days Mrs. Davis was not pessimistic about the future. "She was able to tolerate pain in her back with the aid of narcotic drugs, but did not have complete relief."

A few days later, Mrs. Davis died as a result of bleeding from an operation intended to stop further spread of her cancer.

Dr. Grof and his colleagues make it very clear that psychedelic treatment of terminal patients does not always end in such encouraging results. Still, the fact that emotional suffering can be eased for a considerable time in some instances will undoubtedly lead to more research.

Time and again, however, physicians involved in this area of treatment warn that drug therapy never has been and never will be the answer to all the problems of terminal care. Too often physicians overuse drugs, or use them without impressive benefit to their patients. The pain-killers become a crutch for the physician instead of a merciful helper to his patient. Indeed, there is considerable belief that the dosage and number of drugs the attending doctor prescribes could almost be used as an indicator of his own comfort or discomfort.

The exact way in which heroin, or other narcotics, and psychedelic drugs block out a terminal patient's pain is not known at present. Physicians using both methods of chemotherapy agree that first, there is bound to be some placebo effect, and second, that psychiatric support is an essential ingredient in the therapy. Indeed it may be *the* essential ingredient. Many doctors remain convinced that such drug therapy alone is not appropriate and that "hand holding," intense care, and frank discussions are the best way of comforting a dying person. Dr. Austin Kutscher, a leader in the "study of death" movement, notes, however, that "there aren't nearly enough hand holders around. In the absence of those who know how to help the terminal patient die well, LSD and heroin therapy may, after further study, prove to be a distinctly desirable alternative."

> "All the doctors!—helpless flies now, climbing across the granite face of death."
>
> *John Gunther,* DEATH BE NOT PROUD

5

DOCTORS AND DEATH

A thought that most doctors express when they talk about death is the fine line that divides it from life. "Life one moment, death the next."

Doctors understand that there is far more to a human being than simply his physical makeup. One moment the doctor sees and talks to a person who is alive, rational, able to converse. He is warm, breathing, his heart beats. The next moment that living, thinking being is nothing more than an aggregate of organic material. Something has been removed from the organism, but nothing visible has left it.

The fine line between life and death is something that physicians, even with their extensive knowledge of the human body, seem unable to comprehend or explain. One doctor recalls an experience when he was an intern, working in the emergency room of a city hospital. A man was brought in. His wife had just discovered that he had been unfaithful to her. Furious with jealousy the woman emptied a gun into him point blank, leaving six bullet holes in his anterior chest. By a quirk of luck each bullet had apparently struck a rib and traveled around under the skin. The wounds were only superficial and the doctors removed the bullets in a relatively simple procedure. The man walked away alive, and suffered no aftereffects. "If any one of those bullets had gone straight through his chest he would have been killed," the doctor says.

The next week the same physician was again on emergency room duty when one of the hospital nurses brought in her young child. He was dead on arrival. The youngster had reached up to the kitchen table and knocked off a cup and saucer. A small piece of porcelain chipped from the cup and hit him in the neck, severing the child's jugular vein.

"It was a tiny gash, no more than a fourth of an inch long, but in the right place, and that was it," the physician muses, still shaking his head over the incidents even though they occurred nearly a quarter-century before. "One man is hit in the chest by six bullets and nothing happens. A child has a scratch that anywhere else could be handled by a Band-Aid, but it clips his jugular vein and he is dead. Life one moment, death the next."

Stories such as these are familiar to most physicians, who are expected to retain their composure no matter how dramatic or tragic the case might be. As Sir William Osler has noted, the physician must have "coolness and presence of mind . . . clearness of judgment in moments of grave peril. . . . The physician who has the misfortune to be without it [imperturbability], who betrays indecision and worry and shows that he is flustered and flurried . . . loses rapidly the confidence of his patients."

From the very beginning of their medical training, students are tutored in these attributes. Many adjust to the ordeal, but more than one would-be physician has decided to change his profession when, in medical school, he found that he could not cope with certain of his responsibilities.

During the first year of medical school, the student's first professional encounter with the dead is the cadaver in his anatomy course. The dissection is a mechanical process. The cadaver is not really thought of as a human being; its name is unknown, as is its background. Any relationship between the cadaver, the medical student, life, and death is really unimportant. It is difficult to conceive of the cadaver as having lived at all. To the students the cadaver is as impersonal as a machine. Like plumbers or electricians, medical students must become completely familiar with all of its circuits, tubes, pipes, and connections, if they are to learn from the dead how to repair the living.

In the second year of medical school every student observes his first autopsy and for the first time in his medical life he will associate a corpse with a living person. The student will examine the person's medical record up to the time of death, which may have occurred only hours before. He will talk to the physician who attended the patient, and he will hear of the course of the fatal illness. This can be a trying experience, as witnessed by the recollections of one physician, who as a second-year medical student had to perform his first autopsy on a two-year-old child.

"For me to see this two-year-old child dead, and perform an autopsy on him was one of the most nerve-racking things I have ever done in my life. I went back home after that and I don't think I did anything or went anywhere for several days. Then I talked at length to an older friend. He made me see that this was the sort of thing I would have to put up with and I was able to come to grips and seek peace with myself and I stayed on in medical school. I vowed at that time, though, never to become a pediatrician. I remember thinking that I might be able to take death in an older person, but I certainly wasn't going to be able to watch young children die."

As the medical student completes the first four years of his formal medical education he must begin to make decisions concerning his future as a physician. Today more than 80 per cent of medical school graduates enter specialties. The specialty that a physician chooses dictates, to a large degree, what his experiences with death will be. His anticipation may be a very important factor in helping the future doctor to determine his field of interest. The pathologist, for example, will rarely examine living patients, spending his time in the laboratory and in the morgue; the neurosurgeon, however, will have frequent contact with dying patients and they will often be young persons who

107

die from traumatic injuries. Physicians who enter areas such as pediatrics, internal medicine, and obstetrics, which provide primary patient care, are entering specialties where death is a less frequent occurrence, but when it does occur it can be a profoundly disturbing event.

While dermatologists, ophthalmologists, and endocrinologists may never encounter death in their practices, surgeons must constantly deal with the possibility. Even one of the most elementary surgical procedures, the appendectomy, carries the risk of death of 0.5 per cent. "There is a lot of luck to surgery," Dr. Charles Mayo has pointed out. "Not long ago, I had 103 consecutive cases without an operative or postoperative death. Then I had three deaths in a week." The surgeon, however, frequently does not have the close relationship with his patients that primary care physicians do.

Still, many surgeons become very disturbed upon the death of one of their patients. In his book *Hearts,* Thomas Thompson notes, for example, that Dr. Michael DeBakey takes death as "an intolerable almost personal affront to his skill, to his very being. On the rare occasion that patients died on his table, he would cancel the rest of the day's schedule, stalk to his office, shut the door, lock it, and stay inside for hours."

In the specialty of psychiatry, practitioners may rarely experience the death of a patient, but they will certainly be involved with the threat of death in the case of potentially self-destructive patients.

By the time a physician has completed medical school and entered his internship he may have already resolved many of his ambiguities about death. But most doctors admit that they never really adjust to losing a patient.

While he was a senior intern in obstetrics, one physician recalls that he delivered a woman of a stillborn baby. "The baby had apparently been alive until a day or two—maybe an hour—prior to delivery, but the umbilical cord had become wrapped around its neck and the baby was born dead. I was shaken up very badly and went in to tell this woman about what had happened.

"She ended up comforting me. This mother who had just had a stillborn child was comforting me who was supposed to be the doctor. I was trying to explain to her about the baby dying and she was comforting me, explaining that these things did happen. She had several other children and faced the facts of life better than I did."

With this information about individual physicians' attitudes and experiences, it is not difficult to see why different physicians treat terminal patients in different ways. Should the doctor be blunt or ambiguous in discussing the patient's prognosis with him? At the very least, most agree that whatever the approach, a physician should never tell a dying patient that he has only six weeks, or six months, or any finite time to live. The reasons for this are several. First, there is a real fear that with such specific knowledge a patient may give up, or attempt to commit suicide. Second, of course, a physician simply may have no way of telling how long a person has to live, and the possibility of spontaneous remission of a disease always exists. Finally, there is the always possible chance that a cure will be found.

For these reasons some physicians still adhere to the "say nothing" philosophy, although this practice has been criticized by those who are becoming increasingly involved with the dying patient and his world. Statistics show that between 69 and 90 per cent of physicians—depending on the study—favor a conspiracy of silence regarding their fatally ill patients. Ironically, however, between 77 and 89 per cent of the patients—again depending on the study— want to know the truth. It is speculated that the common medical practice in such instances may be influenced by the anxieties of the healthy, in this case the doctor, instead of the wishes of the seriously ill and the dying. Ask a doctor whether he would want to know if he was suffering from a terminal illness and he would probably say "yes." It is the same physician, however, who often cannot face the idea of talking frankly with a dying patient or his family.

Does the person suffering from a fatal illness want to be told? He may have never discussed this important matter with his family. When he becomes ill, it can be difficult to elicit an answer. If the person has expressed a desire to know then the physician should be informed, for it may make it easier for him to cope with the situation when it arises.

In a study of dying and mourning behavior, British anthropologist Geoffrey Gorer noted that all nineteen patients in his survey who died of cancer had been kept in ignorance about their prognosis. He reported a great deal of regret and bitterness concerning this among the bereaved and noted that good marriage relationships had often been reduced to "unkindness and falsity" by such deception. On the other hand, in another British study, psychiatrist John Hinton learned that a large majority of more than one hundred dying patients in a general hospital ward knew that death was imminent, even though they hadn't been told.

The facts brought out by such studies are fascinating and frightening, for it appears that the very truths from which the patient is being protected are the same truths that he is being forced to live with, and quite alone. It does not seem prudent to suggest that a universal system of informing patients should be instituted, but it is evident that there is a great need for a reconsideration of the various factors involved in helping to ease the fear, alienation, and loneliness of the terminally ill.

In attempting to obtain patients for a study of dying behavior, psychiatrist Herman Feifel ran into serious obstacles, not from the patients, but from his fellow physicians. "Isn't it cruel, sadistic, and traumatic to discuss death with seriously ill and terminally ill people?" doctors asked him.

Feifel was able to overcome such objections only after he was allowed to interview and test two small groups of seriously ill patients. He recalls that "not only were there no untoward incidents, but an unanticipated felicitous byproduct was the seeming psychotherapeutic effect on some of the patients as a result of discussing their attitudes toward death."

Eventually, his study progressed and Feifel found that 82 per cent of his sample of sixty terminally ill patients wanted to be told about their condition in order to facilitate carrying out personal tasks. Representative statements were, "Settle my affairs," "Make various financial and family arrangements," as well as simply because "It's my life—I have a right to know," or "Would respond to treatment better if actually knew what I was up against," and

"Would have time to live with the idea and learn to die."

Dr. L. Beaty Pemberton, assistant professor of surgery at Emory University Medical School, believes that each time the diagnosis of a terminal illness is made the dilemma that faces the physician becomes an ethical question because it contains both the freedom to make the decision and the responsibility for it. Dr. Pemberton contends that there are four basic reasons to support a patient's right to the truth. First, the patient must be recognized as a person with human moral quality; for, without knowledge, responsibility, and freedom the individual may fail to come to grips with his situation. The second reason is that the patient has a right to know about his disease; even though he entrusts his health to the physician, the facts of his condition are his own property. Third, the patient has a right to know because the doctor-patient relationship is a personal one based upon mutual respect and confidence. A physician's lies can "produce great anxiety in the patient and he develops a fear of the unknown and fear of the truth," Dr. Pemberton says. Finally, the patient has a right to know the truth about his own condition because he alone knows his obligations, the responsibilities he must discharge if faced with a life-threatening situation.

In a survey by the physcians' newspaper, *Chronic Disease Management,* doctors responded to questions regarding informing patients about terminal illness in varying ways. A Chicago doctor wrote, "I tell all my terminal patients their diagnosis as early as possible—my only exceptions being the very senile or psychotic. This makes for a more comfortable course for the patient as well as a better relationship with the family and the personnel who must provide care." Another physician commented that "What to tell the patient depends entirely upon the patient's need to know and the family's desire—every case is different. Frequently, both doctor and patient know and both 'play the game' without being brutal about it."

Many physicians believe that when the patient is ready to know about his condition, he will ask questions. Then, after assimilating what he can, the patient will proceed to further questions and discussions. In other cases the family may not want the patient to know about his condition.

111

In such circumstances the physician must weigh both sides of the issue and use his best judgment, although he will probably go along with the family's wishes.

Surely the truth can often be brutal, cold, and cruel. It can, on the other hand, also be gentle, merciful, and hopeful. When a physician discusses a patient's condition with him the discussion must be suited to the patient's needs and character. The doctor must be guided by his patient.

One reason frequently cited for the reluctance of many physicians to disclose impending death is that the social and psychological problems of the patient may be most acute when he knows he is dying. Nevertheless, most physicians believe that if the patient really wants to know, he will somehow learn the truth without being told outright. Some doctors will even maneuver their conversations with patients so as to disclose the facts indirectly. Whatever the case, however, an individual's actual "awareness" of his own condition is of utmost importance in influencing what happens to the patient and his family, and the way in which doctors and nurses give him care.

The "awareness" of dying theory proposed by San Francisco sociologists Barney G. Glaser and Anselm L. Strauss has received a good deal of attention in the last decade. Glaser and Strauss believe that there are four possible situations, or awareness contexts, in which a terminal patient, family, and hospital personnel can relate. These are closed awareness, suspected awareness, mutual pretense awareness, and open awareness.

Closed awareness is the situation in which the patient does not know about his impending death, although relatives and hospital personnel do. This is fairly common, for, after all, modern hospitals themselves are designed to keep information (on charts and records, for example) away from the patient and his family. Staff members guard against displaying their own reactions to a patient's impending death, although they often relay clues to the dying. Nurses may begin spending less time with a patient, talk little with him, or request an assignment elsewhere. Physicians tend to discuss cases with each other in a conference room, out of hearing range and sight of the patient, or, perhaps discuss his problem in medical jargon he can't understand alongside his bed. Family members, too, seem to deliberately guard the "secret" that a relative is dying. It is interesting to contrast such situations with the routine practice in some Asian countries where the relatives of a patient gather around his hospital bed a few days before the expected death, thus indicating to him that they are there to help reassure and comfort him, and keep him company during his passage.

In the closed awareness situation the patient has no say in the matter of his own demise. Whether or not he is lucid, he is deemed incapable of, or unwilling to receive such knowledge. Indeed, for a person who has led a full and intelligent life, this is undoubtedly a difficult situation in which to be placed.

Sometimes overlapping with closed awareness is suspicion awareness, which can be compared to a competition between the patient and medical personnel. The patient may keep testing staff members, who will remain on the defensive. In this situation the patient does not know he is dying, he only suspects it. Such situations may lead to mistrust of physicians or nurses and can give rise to serious problems.

For the patient who is dying the dangers of suspicion awareness are easy to imagine. A patient may die without ever confirming suspicions. He may never have taken such precautions as drawing up a will or having personal talks with relatives, who may become depressed as a result. A patient's spirits can also fluctuate greatly because of the anxieties generated by his suspicions.

On the other hand, patients may believe they have a terminal illness when they do not. This problem can be complicated if the person's illness calls for medical procedures that seem to be unusual or life threatening. Persuading such a patient that he is going to recover may be especially difficult when he has watched doctors and nurses deliberately deceive other patients who were actually dying.

The mutual pretense stage of awareness is the situation in which the patient, staff, and family members all know the patient is dying, but each pretends the other is ignorant of the facts. Such games may seem absurd, but they can offer the patient both dignity and privacy, although they deprive him of closer relationships with family or staff.

One terminal patient said that when her family and husband insisted on pretending that she would recover, she suffered from the isolation and felt as if she were trapped in giant rolls of cotton. However, when the patient himself initiates the mutual pretense awareness it may offer relief to family members and personnel by minimizing embarrassment. "But for closer kin," Glaser and Strauss say, "franker concourse may have many advantages."

The "franker concourse" is a situation of open awareness, where all parties involved know that the patient is dying and openly acknowledge it in their behavior. Open awareness offers the patient a chance to end his life according to his own thoughts and ideas about the proper way to die. He has the opportunity to try to finish important work, make the proper farewells, and detail his wishes for his estate. Furthermore Glaser and Strauss believe that a person "dying in an acceptable manner" has a better chance of receiving cooperation from hospital staff in the management of his death.

Another facet of open awareness is the close relationship that can develop between the hospital staff and the patient. Many nurses, for example, derive deep satisfaction from working with the dying. Nurses often relate how they have talked at length with a patient during the time before his death, and listened while he talked about his own life. Such sympathetic discussions are undoubtedly of great comfort to the patient as well.

In addition to making a last illness less difficult for the patient, open awareness helps the family by reducing much of the strain and secrecy that would accompany other stages of awareness. In this situation the relatives may be able to share a person's last thoughts and moments with him—a mutually beneficial relationship. It should be noted, however, that some persons simply cannot carry on conversations with relatives or friends they know are going to die shortly.

Dying patients can progress from one stage of awareness to another, or combine one or more stages. A patient, for example, may be willing to discuss his death with a physician or nurse, but be unable to admit his knowledge to a wife or child. In some cases he might even be sure his family knows about his condition, but not broach the subject for fear of informing and upsetting them.

The opportunity to discuss one's own impending death with a physician may be important for another reason. There is a widely proposed theory that a strong fear of death itself exists among some people who become physicians. The choice of medicine as a career, according to psychiatrist C. W. Wahl, "sometimes may represent a counterphobic defense against death, a reaction formation to an earlier fear, mastered by doing the very thing that was previously frightening. It serves sometimes to represent a kind of identification with the aggressor, a wish to be on the winning team."

Theorizing that the reason why certain physicians enter medicine is to control and govern their own strong fears of death, Dr. Herman Feifel conducted a pilot study on the attitudes of forty physicians. The results indicated that medical doctors thought less about death than did two control groups, one of patients and one of professionals. On the other hand, the doctors were more afraid of death than either of the control groups. In another study Feifel compared eighty-one physicians, ninety-five healthy normal persons, and ninety-two patients—fifty-two of whom were seriously ill and knew they might die and forty terminally ill who knew they must die as a result of their disease. Again he found that the physicians were "significantly more afraid of death than both the physically sick and healthy, normal groups." The major reason cited for these fears among doctors was a personal accident, illness, or threat of death before the age of five, compared to a similar threat between ages six and twelve for patients and healthy normal persons.

The physicians were significantly less religious in outlook concerning their personal fate after death than were the control groups, and their perception of death was basically materialistic: Death was viewed as the end of the process of life with no continuation in another time or place. Answering a question concerning how they would spend their time with only six months to live, physicians most commonly responded that they would "continue on as usual."

Certainly it seems logical to assume that the fear of death in some physicians has given them an overwhelming desire to do combat with it. Medical training, in fact, reinforces this attitude. The doctor's role is one of authority and power. He is taught to manipulate life's processes and do what can be done to triumph over death. The physician's challenge and his satisfaction come largely from winning this battle and effecting cures.

The age of the physician also apparently has a great deal to do with the way in which he views death. Young doctors and nurses are likely to react to death with outrage, refusing to consider it inevitable. They tend to utilize excessively vigorous treatment in an attempt to delay it. The middle-aged physician is more likely to face up to the fact of death with an intellectual acceptance coupled with emotional detachment, and the elderly physician is likely to remain calmer, with a greater personal acceptance of death.

If the doctor himself has an above average fear of death he may become extremely anxious when confronted with it, such as when he diagnoses a fatal illness in a patient. To cope with his own anxiety the physican may seem excessively hopeful in discussions with the family, thus making their adjustment to the reality more difficult. Instead the physician's goal should be to assure the family that everything possible is being done for the patient, and at the same time approach the situation in a realistic manner, offering the family an opportunity to prepare for their loss. Unfortunately, training in psychological aspects of dealing with the dying and their families has been conspicuously absent in the past and only recently has begun to play a part in medical training in some medical schools.

"I must admit," says Dr. Louis R. Zako, a family physician from Michigan, "that when the anxiety, the fear provoked within me as the physician becomes too great, it's very, very comfortable to deal with the dying process on a technical level. Because then there is no real involvement. There have been times when I haven't been able to cope with an individual patient in a terminal situation, and in a cowardly way, I have run to the stereotyped role of myself as a scientist and technical expert, who doesn't concern himself with people's feelings. Certainly, depending upon

116

the individual physician, some may find the anxiety so great that they always deal with it in this way."

To help physicians learn more about death and dying, and to help them cope better with the many anxieties involved, a number of individuals have formed action organizations. A new medical subspecialty called thanatology (from the Greek word *thanatos,* meaning "death") has come into being. The Foundation of Thanatology was founded in 1967 by four professors at the Columbia University College of Physicians and Surgeons. The nonprofit organization has an advisory board of more than one hundred medical professionals (as well as advisors in related fields); it holds regular workshops and seminars, conducts research, and publishes three journals: *Archives of the Foundation of Thanatology, Journal of Thanatology,* and *Bereavement and Allied Fields.* The foundation has already produced a number of books based upon papers given as its various symposia.

The guiding spirit behind the organization is its president Dr. Austin Kutscher, an associate professor at Columbia University School of Dental and Oral Surgery. Kutscher was led to his interest in thanatology by a personal experience, the death of his wife. The dentist found that he and his family were almost totally unprepared to face the tragedy. He also learned, to his dismay, that his physician and psychiatrist colleagues could offer little help and comfort either during his wife's terminal illness or after her death in 1967. Today Dr. Kutscher's second wife, as well as his sons, are important organizers and workers in the foundation.

Another indication that the study of death and the dying is gaining in importance in scientific circles occurred in 1970, when a symposium, "Problems in the Meaning of Death," was a part of the program at the annual meeting of the American Association for the Advancement of Science. The session was sponsored and organized by the Institute of Society, Ethics and the Life Sciences, a nonprofit, foundation-supported center established in 1969 at Hastings-on-Hudson, New York.

The Hastings Center, as it is called, has task force groups which deal with topical aspects of many areas of ethics, biology, and medicine. Their task force on death and dying is the center of an ongoing research program, funded in part by the Ford Foundation, "inquiring into the adequacy of present definitions of death, current medical practices in the care of the dying patient, professional and legislative codes pertaining to death, and present philosophical and theological understandings of the meaning of death." Members of the task force include some of the nation's most eminent scientists, physicians, theologians, and lawyers, who meet two or three times a year to discuss current issues and assign research topics to group members.

One member of the task force has herself functioned much as a total organization in encouraging interest in the subject of death. Referred to by some as the "Ralph Nader of the terminally ill," Swiss-born psychiatrist Elisabeth Kübler-Ross seems to be continually moving around the country lecturing to medical professionals and laymen alike. The large audiences of doctors, nurses, and medical students attending her lectures is indicative of the growing interest and concern over the subjects of death and dying.

Courses or symposia on death and the dying patient have already been offered at a number of medical and theology schools, and as general courses at some universities and colleges; included among them are Stanford, New York University, Chicago, Oregon, Rochester Institute of Technology, Pennsylvania State, Columbia, Rhode Island, Boston University, Purdue, and Emory. In the spring of 1971 when New York University instituted a course on "The Meaning of Death," there was so much student interest that the course was very quickly oversubscribed. Every semester more professional schools are adding courses or special seminars in which their students can study various aspects of death and dying.

Meanwhile a Duke University internist, Dr. William Poe, has suggested a new medical specialty, marantology (from the Greek word *marantos,* meaning "withered" or "faded"). Marantologists would not resort to heroic measures to keep their patients alive. They would care for the old, the incurable, and those who have "committed the sin of remaining alive but not yielding to our manipulations." The marantologist would be trained to see his patients die without experiencing feelings of guilt or personal failure.

118

"When confronted with losing, we do all kinds of things to prove we are trying to do good. Surgical residents do radical neck dissections on octogenarians. We put feeding tubes in poor old bodies that should be allowed to die. Rehabilitation people break their backs to get old hemiplegics [those paralyzed on one side] to take feeble steps for no purpose," Dr. Poe says.

The new specialty would help people, especially physicians, enduring losing. "It should not use silly euphemisms such as rehabilitation and convalescence for its losing patients. It should not send its dear old people to intensive care units to be treated as winners."

Certainly, though, it would be difficult for a physician to specialize only in death and dying. In a society where the possibility of death is often denied, who would his patients be? Would enough physicians admit defeat by referring "losing" patients to the marantologist? It is obvious that one of the greatest rewards and justifications for a physician is watching his patients recover. Some will die, to be sure, but more will live and become healthy once again. How long could a physician withstand the emotional strain of knowing that each of his patients would die—and soon?

The best answer to these dilemmas lies in more education for all physicians. Just as every doctor specializes in health and life he must, in a special sort of way, also specialize in death.

119

"Doctor, doctor, will I die?
Yes my child and so will I."
Anonymous

———————————

6

CHILDREN AND DEATH

When a member of the immediate family dies, what should a child be told? Should the child be told the facts, lied to a little, or kept from the truth? Does a child comprehend death? Should he mourn with the family? How is he expected to act? These are but a few of the myriad questions regarding death that parents will ask.

If it is difficult for parents, as mature adults, to accept the fact, or inevitability of death, then it is even more difficult for children to comprehend. As has been mentioned, modern ways of living complicate the situation because so many people pass through childhood and adolescence without experiencing the loss by death of a single person close to them. The aged and infirm are put in institutions, and grandparents rarely live under the same roof with grandchildren. The majority of hospitals have strict visiting rules, generally (and perhaps unfortunately) excluding children.

Because of the anxiety about death that adults harbor, they have a strong tendency to shield a child from death and dying. As a rule, however, children are not unnecessarily evasive about discussing death. S. Anthony, a British psychologist, found that many children mentioned death spontaneously. In his study parents made notes of any conversations relevant to the subject. The investigation showed that the children frequently talked about death, and interestingly the comments often came at bathtime. In a more objective portion of the same study, the word *dead* was added to a list of words in a vocabulary test; only two of ninety-one children tested avoided the word deliberately.

Still, adults tend to avoid the subject. They should note, however, that to shield a child from knowing is to shield him from learning, and children must learn. "Actually," says psychiatrist Walter Char of the University of Hawaii Medical School, "it is better at an early age in a normal, matter-of-fact fashion for a child to be exposed to the concept that death is a part of life."

Obviously, age plays an important role in the way a child perceives death. A child's first concept of death is separation; this prevails until about age three. Scientists know that young children exhibit great anxiety over separation from a significant person, even if the separation is brief. The observation of such anxiety only serves to confirm what kind of difficulties a child must undergo when faced with the permanent loss of a person close to him.

Between ages three and five or six, children view death as a temporary situation, like someone resting or taking a trip. In the fantasy world of the three, four, five, and six year old, where a child can magically change the world around him, destroying and reviving people and animals at will, death is perceived as a reversible situation. "I know daddy is dead," said a five year old, "but why doesn't he come home for dinner?" Although death is a relatively clear concept for children of this age it simply is not perceived as a permanent happening. In a lecture, Dr. Elisabeth Kübler-Ross recalled a personal situation to illustrate. When her four-year-old daughter helped her bury the family's pet dog in the backyard, the child told her famous psychiatrist-mother, "Mommy, it's not really so sad. Next spring when your tulips come up, he'll come up again and play with me."

In his book *The Emerging Personality,* Dr. George E.

Gardner warns that "the fear of separation is one of the most basic fears of all children." The difference between "gone and coming back" and "gone and never coming back" should be made very clear to children, for this is a vital element in a child's anxiety. When death is explained on this basis, the child psychiatrist adds, "considerable emphasis should be placed upon reassurance of the child about his own security." In other words the child must be helped to understand that he will not be left alone with no one to care for him. It may take the child under six years old a week or more to discard fantasies of the return of the dead person.

Up to about age ten, most children visualize death as a bogeyman, a skeleton, or an eerie ghost dressed in white. By about age ten children are usually able to understand that "death" is not a person and can formulate realistic concepts based on biological principles. But unless parents and teachers discuss death candidly with them, children cannot learn that to die is final. Some professionals simply suggest that parents answer all of a child's questions about death directly and honestly. Often talking about what has happened to a dead pet or animal will make the experience an easier one to explain and understand.

Too many loving parents, in their haste to save their children from all things that may be unpleasant, try to protect them from pain and grief. If a pet turtle or goldfish dies it is hurriedly replaced with a new one, in the hope that the child will not notice the difference. If a pet dog, cat, or bird dies, parents rush to replace it with "nicer" and more expensive animals.

What, though, are the lessons that a child learns from early experiences of loss of this type? Will a youngster conclude, perhaps, that the loss of a close relative or friend is not of great importance—that the emotion of love, which has been fostered in him from birth, can be turned off and on, transferred quickly, and loyalties easily switched?

"A child should not be deprived of his right to grieve and to mourn. He should be free to feel sorrow in the loss of someone loved. The child's humanity is deepened, and his character ennobled, when he can lament the end of life

122

and love," says Dr. Haim Ginott, author of *Between Parent and Child.*

The loss of a pet is a beautiful opportunity for open and direct discussion of the subject of death. The child may be encouraged to talk about his personal thoughts and feelings and to ask questions. If a child sees that adults are comfortable about discussing death with him, then he himself will be more at ease in talking or thinking about it, which he inevitably will.

When parents insist on replacing a child's pet without telling the child, it can cause confusion and emotional pain. Six-year-old Suzy's cat was run over and killed while the girl was visiting her grandmother for the day. Her father rushed out to the local pound and was lucky enough, he thought, to find a cat almost exactly like Taffy. The body of the old cat was disposed of, and the new Taffy took its place in the house.

That evening, after Suzy had returned home, she noticed no difference in her pet. But after dinner when she tried to cuddle and play with it, the cat ran away from her. "Taffy doesn't love me, she won't play," the girl complained.

"Of course she loves you. She will play," answered the father. When Suzy finally caught up with the substitute Taffy, and tried to hold the cat in her arms, she was bitten and scratched on the face. Her cuts required stitches, the parent suffered guilt and anguish that would not have been necessary, and the new Taffy was banished to the pound. The girl was never told what had actually happened.

In general, wise parents realize that children should not be excluded from sharing grief and sorrow any more than they should be from sharing joy and happiness in the course of normal family relationships. When a death in the family occurs, and a child is not told exactly what has happened, he may become confused and feel great anxiety. He may fill his knowledge gap with figments of his imagination, usually far more bizarre than the truth could ever be, and more frightening to the child. These childhood fantasies can be carried into maturity.

"Children are excluded from the planning and sharing

123

of sadness on the pretext that it would be too much for them. But the result is not protection. They are denied a potentially beautiful experience that can unify and strengthen a family," says Dr. Ross.

A frequently asked question in this context is "Should we take the child to the funeral?" According to the Rev. Edgar Jackson, who has written extensively on religion and psychological experience, "Children love a parade, and a funeral is a private family parade from the deathbed to the hole in the ground, or crematorium.

"If a child wants to participate in this significant family event, he should be allowed to. I think more children have been damaged by exclusion than by inclusion, because they will accept [the funeral] at the point at which they are able."

Dr. Herman Feifel believes that denying a child the right to attend a funeral tends to reflect the anxieties and concerns of the adult rather than the child's actual ability to cope with the situation. By attending the funeral, too, the reality of the situation will be reinforced in the child's mind, thus preventing him from developing unrealistic ideas or fears about the death of a loved one.

Professionals generally agree that if the child is old enough to understand what is taking place, he should be offered the opportunity to take part in the ceremony marking the end of the life of a person who was close to him. Young children who are too fidgety should probably not be permitted to attend, but older children may be encouraged—*but never forced*—to attend the service. A child who resists going to the funeral should not be made to feel guilty. His questions about the ceremonies should be answered in a straightforward and truthful manner and he may be told that if he wishes he can go to the cemetery to visit the grave later.

Children who remain at home can participate in various ways in the final rites. They can answer the door, unwrap flowers, and help in the kitchen. Children may derive a great deal of comfort from ritual, and although they may not completely understand, they are likely to be affected by the sense of peace and order and the feeling that the everyday routine goes on.

A parent or relative should not be distressed that a child attending a funeral will witness crying and grieving, for it is at times like these that a child learns that having and expressing such feelings are normal. The facts of life, in fact, are that adults do cry.

"The first step in helping children face their loss is to allow them to express fully their fears, fantasies and feelings," says Dr. Ginott. "Comfort and consolation come from sharing deep emotions with a listener who cares. The parents may also put into words some of the feelings that a child is bound to have, but may find difficult to express."

For example, if the child's mother has died the father might say to him, "You miss mommy, don't you? You loved her a lot, and so did I. She loved you. You wish she were still with us. It is hard to believe that she is dead. We will remember her forever."

Like the adult, the child has a need to work through his grief and anxieties. He should share his feelings, both positive and negative, about the deceased with the family. His recollections of the dead person should be encouraged as should participation in discussions with the family about the future. Neither children nor adults can grieve normally without such an outward expression of sorrow as well as the sympathy, support, and understanding of others.

If children are not allowed to share grief and sadness, serious emotional problems can arise. When five-and-a-half-year-old Tony's mother suddenly died he was sent to stay with relatives until after the funeral. No explanation was given. When his father came for him a week later, Tony was told that he would never see his mother again because she had gone to heaven. The boy began to question his father, but he noticed that the questions made his father extremely uncomfortable. Confused, the youngster ceased his questioning. He became afraid of strangers, began to wet his bed and wake up with nightmares. Tony had to be taken out of kindergarten because of uncontrollable temper tantrums, and he would never ride in a car without his father. With time these symptoms subsided, but years later Tony became a very depressed person.

Another example was eight-year-old Bernie, who appeared not to show any grief when his father was killed in an accident. The first week after the tragedy the boy was unusually cheerful. He did not cry, ask questions, or want to go to the funeral. In spite of his sister's weeping and his mother's attempts to explain the accident, the boy stopped talking about his father altogether. Fully twelve years later, in therapy after two attempts to kill himself, it became clear that Bernie's problems were linked to his deep attachment to his father and his unwillingness to give him up.

Often a parent may become too dependent on children after the loss of a spouse, and this too can prevent proper grieving in children. When Tom was thirteen, his father died of a heart attack. The youngster was forced to play a supportive role because initially his mother could not cope with the loss. For weeks she was all but incapacitated, and unable to help her two young daughters. Tom made the funeral arrangements and comforted his sisters and mother.

"Everyone cried on my shoulder," he recalls. "By the time they were through and I wanted to mourn, it seemed inappropriate."

Children, in other words, should be allowed to remain children, even though they must be spoken to frankly and honestly. British anthropologist Geoffrey Gorer, among others, has observed that repression of a topic often masks an underlying preoccupation with it. This was the case with sex in the Victorian era and may be true about death in the twentieth century. Modern parents who speak openly with their children about sex, deploring parents who refuse to do so, often avoid the mention of death or try to disguise the subject if it does happen to arise. "The Victorians may well have terrified children with their realistic descriptions of dying and death and with their details of God and of hell and heaven," says British pediatrician Dr. Simon Yudkin, "but we allow them to be terrified by our secrecy and by our private and often furtive misery."

A child may feel a profound sense of shame or guilt throughout his early life if a parent or sibling has died. While most youngsters have lost grandparents or other older relatives, it is not as common for a child to have lost a parent, brother, or sister. My own mother died of leukemia when I was very young, before I knew her, really, and my father remarried several years later. Even though my new mother was actually the only mother I had ever known, I did know that my natural mother had died.

I remember that I was very conscious of this in my elementary school days and it was only in my late teens that I was able, to my great relief, to discuss the fact that my mother had died. It was almost as if I, or my family, had committed an unsociable act by my mother's death. My wife, too, lost her father when she was very young, and in the process of writing this book we discussed our feelings about the parental deaths and the situations in our elementary school years. She commented that she had the same feelings of shame and guilt. "Perhaps," she said, "this is because children are very sensitive to belonging to and being exactly like their peer group. Any difference in family structure sets them apart. Moreover death to us then, and still today, is something that was hushed and not spoken about— a great mystery to a child, which could cause him to become a subject of curiosity to his friends."

These very personal examples illustrate to a great extent why it is important not only for parents to be honest and open with their children in discussing death, but for teachers to discuss the phenomenon with equal candor with their classes. Naturally discussion of death in the classroom is controversial—as has been the discussion of sex. Nevertheless in a large elementary school classroom, where many children own pets or study live animals in the classroom, and where elementary books touching on the subject are available, the discussion can be accomplished in a simple, matter-of-fact way that should not be offensive. Such discussions would certainly offer great consolation to the child who has, or will, lose a loved one, and save him much unnecessary guilt and shame.

The easiest way for a parent to explain the death of a relative to a young child is through the use of euphemisms. Such simplistic talk, however, should be avoided. Even though many have the feeling that a half-truth will upset a child less than facts, few children older than two actually believe such white lies, which may actually confuse instead of comfort.

When one four year old was told that her grandfather had "gone to his eternal sleep," she asked whether he had

127

taken his pajamas with him. She was also very worried that her grandfather might have been angry with her because she had not told him good night before he left. In considering such explanations, it is also crucial for the parent to realize that the child himself must go to sleep every night. Will he, after such an explanation, willingly do so without severe anxiety?

When a five year old was told that "Grandmother went to heaven and became an angel," he prayed that he and the rest of his family would die soon and become angels too.

Another child, a little boy, had just lost his mother. The child had been told, "She went up to the sky." When the boy later flew from his home in North Carolina to Washington, D.C. to visit psychiatrist Dr. Bennett Olshaker, the boy told him that during his flight he had looked "on every cloud, but I didn't see her." The boy was very sad and disappointed, but from what he had been told about his mother's death, his was a reasonable expectation. He had not attended the funeral and had been kept busy elsewhere by well-meaning relatives who wanted to spare him the unhappiness.

Often religious concepts can be of help in telling a child about death. Even parents who do not espouse organized religion and beliefs may encourage their children to retain belief in God when learning about death. When a mother has died, for example, a sensitive father might explain to the child that "Mommy is dead, and her body is buried in the ground (or cremated) but her soul has gone up to heaven." He might also add that his and his child's thoughts and memories will help mommy's soul live on, too.

Dr. Robert Furman, of Cleveland's Center for Research in Child Development, however, gives firm warning that it sometimes seems as if "the surest way to make a confirmed atheist of a young child may be to tell him of a God who takes from him the ones he loves; the surest way to frighten a young child about religious concepts may be to tell him of an ill-defined place where everyone goes after death."

Dr. Furman cites the case of a mother who complained that her four year old had a hard time falling asleep. At bedtime the boy demanded that all the windows be locked, even in summer, and when he was outside he refused to cross streets or to leave the shade of trees. A psychiatrist learned that when the boy's infant brother had died, the child was told that "God had reached down from heaven and while his brother slept had picked him up and taken him to heaven."

If told such things about a dead father, a child could easily live in constant fear that his father would reach down from his mysterious place in the sky to punish him for misbehaving.

Upon reading the above examples, the well-meaning parent will rightly ask, "Then what should I tell the child? What can I say?" There is no simple answer. Many factors should be considered before giving a sensible answer to children's questions about death. And *sensible* is the key word.

"I have come to the conclusion that there is no single explanation of death that will be wholly satisfactory or that should be given to every child," says Dr. George Gardner.

"Always," says the *Gesell Institute's Book of Child Behavior,* "you should answer any questions clearly, directly and truthfully as you can. But not in too great or burdensome detail. If he wants to know more, he will ask further questions."

When a child is simply and honestly told the truth, accompanied by a loving caress, he is reassured. Actions, after all, speak louder than words and while what is said to a child will help him to some extent, how it is said will affect him much more deeply.

Dr. Benjamin Spock advises that the first explanation of death should be "casual, not too scarey. You might say, 'Everybody has to die someday. Most people die when they get very old and tired and weak and they don't want to stay alive any more.' " He urges parents not to convey a feeling of dread when talking about death. "Remember to hug him and smile at him and remind him that you're going to be together for years and years."

It is inevitable that a young child will feel partially or fully responsible when he loses a parent or sibling. Psychiatrists tell us that there is scarcely a person who, in his younger life, did not wish his mother or father or brother to drop dead during a moment of anger or frustration.

"This means," says Dr. Elisabeth Kübler-Ross, "you are a very bad mommy and I make you dead now. But two hours later when I want the peanut butter and jelly sandwich I make you get up again and fix it for me."

But if a child wishes his mother to drop dead and then she really dies, the little one always feels that he has actually killed her. Not only will he feel guilty, but he will also feel terribly deserted and frightened or angry that "mommy does not come back to fix my peanut butter and jelly sandwich." The child also will inevitably look expectantly toward the punishment which must follow the crime. "These are the children who you see fifty or sixty years later who have an abnormal fear of death. Maybe they have to suffer for a good reason," Dr. Ross says.

During a 1972 lecture to nurses at Babies Hospital in New York, the Chicago psychiatrist recalled an experience that perfectly illustrates such a situation. She had, she said, given a lecture in Madison, Wisconsin, where she had asked a standard question to her audience in discussing death and dying. "Is there anybody in the room who didn't ever wish mommy to drop dead?"

"One nun kept looking at me throughout the entire rest of the lecture. I had a strong urge to go up to her and tell her, 'I read you. What is it that you're trying to say?' "

After the lecture the nun lingered and Dr. Ross approached her. She was told by the nun, "I have to write you a letter."

Several days later a "most beautiful" letter arrived at Dr. Ross's office. "The nun wrote that a very peculiar thing had happened to her today. She saw a sign in her hospital that there was to be a lecture on dying and she had a strong urge that she had a calling from God that she had to go to this lecture. For the first time in her life she was aggressive and she demanded that she be chosen as a delegate from her hospital. She was allowed to go and she knew that something very special would happen to her.

"During the lecture, when I asked that question, she had a flash back to something that had happened to her when she was four years old—forty-nine years before, something she had completely forgotten."

In the letter to Dr. Ross the nun recalled that she was the youngest of several children. All of her brothers and sisters were away at school one day and she was playing alone at home. She remembered that her mother called from the bedroom: "Honey, bring me a glass of water." As a typical four year old who didn't want to be bothered, she ignored the call and continued to play. The second time her mother's voice came, "If you don't bring me a glass of water, I think I'll die." The girl dashed out and brought her mother a glass of water. She promptly forgot the incident.

Two days later the mother became acutely ill, was hospitalized, and died the same day. "And mind you," says Dr. Ross, "never once did this little girl share this incident with any other human being. She only said that she remembered that she was never, never supposed to be happy. She was only supposed to take the skinny and bony piece of meat if there was a choice between a good piece and a skinny piece. And she knew that she had to become a nun and dedicate her life to God.

"She told me that when she came to the workshop and I asked, 'Is there anybody in the room who cannot remember having wished their mommy to drop dead, *this is normal*,' she felt a fantastic weight coming off her chest and suddenly, 'I feel free, free, free, free.' This is typical. Needless to say I am not insinuating that all nuns become nuns because something like this happens, but this is a very beautiful example of what can happen."

Such times of fear, grief, and sorrow are times when somebody must reach out to children and convey to them the fact that wishes do not, cannot kill. Even though the child may not perfectly understand, when he becomes ready to talk he will seek out an older friend or relative with whom to talk. With open discussion needless suffering can be avoided in later years.

Dr. Spock has said, "All healthy people of every age have some degree of fear and resentment of death. There is no way to present the matter to children that will get around this basic human attitude. But if you think of death as something to be met eventually with dignity and fortitude you'll be able to give somewhat the same feeling about it to your child."

It is natural for a child, when his parent has died, to experience feelings of loneliness, abandonment, fear, and even anger. While it is true that in certain cases professional help will be necessary, an understanding adult can do a great deal toward helping allay such fears in the child. Children may not always verbalize their fears. They may attempt to avoid open confrontation that might result in visually upsetting the parent, such as causing a widowed mother to cry. Such a child may act as if nothing has occurred, or as if he really does not care at all. But a child's distress will quickly become evident to a sensitive parent. This distress may manifest itself in a change in normal cooperation, a change in moods, minor physical symptoms such as aches and pains, or inability to sleep or eat, as well as more serious symptoms such as lying, stealing, and bedwetting. The wise parent seeks the causes of such changes in behavior patterns. Following are a few behavior patterns that can be considered as warnings that psychiatric help may be needed for a bereaved child:

The child who appears to show no grief at all may be in trouble and have problems much later in life.

If a child maintains an unshakable fixation on the lost love object, if he continues to believe that the dead person will return for more than a week or so he may need aid to give up his fantasy and deal with the reality of the situation.

If a child ceases to function in school or turns to severe delinquent activities. (Some decline in school work is to be expected, but complete absorption in daydreams is a call for help.)

The child whose anger leads him to strike out at society by stealing or other illegal and unsocial acts also needs help.

A major index of how a child masters his loss is how he feels about the people around him. Educational consultant Anne Watt explains that "If he has been unable to detach his affection from the lost loved one, he may hesitate ever to risk forming another deep attachment. He could grow up sure only of his love for himself and for objects which

132

cannot hurt him by leaving him. He would lack courage to risk developing or sustaining relationships with other people lest they, too, desert him. Before reaching adulthood, children with any of these symptoms would benefit greatly from some type of preventive intervention with a counselor."

It should be made clear, however, that just as adults may react to death with shock and disbelief, so may children. When a child returns almost immediately to play after a death in the family it may seem to be a heartless denial of what has just happened. In fact, though, this is an attempt on the part of the child to return to what is familiar, thus allowing himself time to assimilate what is terrible, new, unfamiliar. If the child is allowed such a retreat it can be beneficial, but parents must watch to see that it does not become too prolonged.

Such adaptive behavior should be distinguished from the child pretending that the death has not occurred at all, a form of denial. One six year old, for example, who had always enjoyed school, lost his mother. The boy stopped bringing home his school papers, he forgot them. The youngster was unable to explain his behavior to his father, but an older brother, overhearing a conversation, said, "I know why. There is no mother home to bring the papers to. It would make him too sad so he forgets them at school." The six year old reluctantly agreed that this was the problem and he soon began bringing his papers home once again.

A child's despair at the loss of a loved one can lead to great anger. "I hate daddy for dying," he might say. Or his anger may be vented on others. It is natural for a child, or any of us for that matter, to become angry when a prized possession is taken away. Anger may not be expressed openly by a bereaved child, but may manifest itself through more frequent fights at school with friends and teachers. It is very important for a child to understand that although the death was nobody's fault, it is normal for him to feel angry about it. He should be helped to realize that his is not abnormal behavior, should not result in guilt, and will pass in time.

The fear of abandonment, or "separation anxiety," is

another situation with which parents must help children deal. "Daddy is dead," said little Bobby, "mommy, will you die too and leave me all alone? Who will then take care of me?"

Children have deep concerns about who will take care of them even while they are growing up and seeking their own independence. The way a parent fosters this growing feeling for independence in the child is important to his emotional balance. To the child, "Who will take care of me?" is a common and legitimate question. Even if it is not asked aloud, it is probably being thought about. Dr. Bennett Olshaker says, "If a child voices concern over whether his remaining parent will die he should be told that, although everyone will die someday, it is likely that the parent will live a long life and that the youngster will no doubt be grown up and have a family of his own by the time his other parent dies."

The child, of course, may answer aloud or to himself, "Yes, but what if you die soon?" This brings up a question to which parents should give careful consideration. What if both parents are killed in a plane, car, or other accident? Who would they select to take care of their children? Who would be willing to accept the task? What arrangements will cause the least amount of disruption in the child's life? It is important for parents to share such information with their children, except for the very young. But it is especially important for those children who have already lost one parent and are afraid of the loss of the surviving one. This information can be very reassuring to the child who is attempting to cope with the fear of abandonment.

Psychiatrists advise, too, that parents with terminal illnesses should not try to "protect" their children with a conspiracy of silence. "Young people," declares Dr. Elisabeth Kübler-Ross, "are rarely fooled. By informing them with the rest of the family, they have much more time to prepare for the death and will be better able to face their own without fear."

Although it is unduly cruel of nature to take a loved one from a child, the death of a child is more of an outrage, an even greater waste. But children do die, and that is a simple, if tragic, fact of life.

When the parents of John, a ten year old with leukemia, were told the diagnosis, they expressed the hope that the facts of the disease and its course would be withheld from the child. The physician agreed, and told the parents to tell friends and relatives that the boy had anemia. Similarly, the boy's questions were answered with honesty, except those relating directly to his condition.

After a few conversations with the doctor, the boy stopped asking about his health and the hospital procedure—a situation, by the way, that the doctor was more than willing to accept. When John was later discharged from the hospital, his parents acted cheerful and treated him as if the illness was cured.

After several months, and several more hospitalizations, the boy was close to death, but the seriousness of his illness was still kept a secret from him. The doctor and the parents felt that the child would suffer needlessly if informed that he had only a short time to live. For his part, John asked no more questions about his illness, and kept conversation on a much lighter level.

When the boy died the parents were relieved that they had successfully kept the diagnosis from their son. After the boy's death, however, the fact that he died of leukemia became known to relatives and friends. Shortly thereafter, one of John's school friends began to boast that he knew what was wrong with John before anybody else did. The teacher told this to John's parents who asked the boy about it. They learned that their son had told his friend that he had leukemia, but made him promise he wouldn't tell anyone about it. With this information the parents realized that because they had been unwilling to discuss the truth, they had forced their son to die very much alone.

When seven-year-old Peggy, who was dying, became suspicious and concerned about other children who "disappeared" from the hospital ward, she tried a "frontal attack." She asked everyone she saw, "What is going to happen to me when I die?"

Her physician answered, "I hear my page."

Her nurse answered, "You're a bad girl, don't talk like that. Just take your medicine and you'll get well."

But her minister replied with a question of his own.

135

"What do you think is going to happen?" The girl answered, "One of these days I will fall asleep and when I wake up I will be with Jesus and my little sister."

"That must be very beautiful," said the minister, and at last the girl was satisfied.

It is not uncommon to keep a terminally ill child ignorant of his condition. To be sure, some children are not mature enough to cope with information about their state of health, but others are very curious and might benefit from simple answers to their questions. Youngsters, however, generally do not ask such questions because those around them forbid it. Because of such taboos on meaningful conversation, children often resort to symbolic—and often nonverbal—language.

An eight-year-old boy with an inoperable brain tumor was very frightened of death. He viewed it as a great destructive force, but was unwilling, or unable to talk about it. Counseling was advised for the youngster, and during one session he was given crayons and paper. He drew a picture of a huge tank with a small boy holding a stop sign in front of its barrel. The tank signified death, the destructive and unstoppable force, and the boy with his stop sign signified his fruitless attempt to halt it. The child's understanding counselor drew another, similar picture, but added a larger boy standing next to the small boy, with his hand on his shoulder. After several more sessions with the counselor, the eight year old eventually came to accept his impending death and he drew another picture. He drew, in black crayon, a large bird with a small touch of bright yellow on one of its wings. He described it as "a bird of peace flying up to the sky with a little bit of sunshine on *my* wing." It was the last picture the boy drew, and he died shortly thereafter. But his doctors, nurses, and parents must have gained comfort in the knowledge that this child had come to understand and accept what he was going through.

Another example illustrates a different kind of indirect communication. A fatally ill eight year old was in an oxygen tent. She had not spoken of death or her illness to anybody, but one night when the nurse was in the room the child asked, "What happens if my oxygen tent catches fire?"

The nurse replied, "It won't, we don't allow anybody to smoke in here." The nurse's reply was understandable, but even as she gave it she realized that the child was reaching out for help and support. Though recognizing the cry for help, the young nurse did not feel that she could handle the situation effectively. She phoned her supervisor, rousing her from bed, and the more experienced nurse also realized that this was a time for action.

The supervisor came to the ward, sat down next to the child and put her shoulder on the child's pillow. She said, "What was it you asked about a fire?" The child threw her arms around the nurse and cried on her shoulder.

"I just know I'm going to die," the child said, "and I've just got to talk to somebody about it." The nurse continued talking to the child, honestly answering her questions, and before the nurse left she asked, "Is there anything else I can help you with?"

The child replied that yes, there was. She wanted the nurse to help her talk about her impending death with her mother, just once.

When the mother came to the hospital the next morning the head nurse called her into her office and explained what had happened. The mother became extremely upset, physically pushed the nurse away and rushed out of the office. After that the mother refused to enter her child's room alone. She was shielding herself, to be certain that the child could not bring up the subject of dying.

The fatally ill child in the hospital situation continually searches for verbal as well as nonverbal clues that can help him cope with his isolation. The child will listen to footsteps, tone of voice, and visually follow visitors around the room. Children detect subtle changes, a mother's tearful expression or the snapping together of a purse before a visitor enters the room.

The fatally ill child's first feelings may be of isolation and loneliness. In very small children, for example, the concept of death is synonymous with separation. "Our biggest hope in such cases," says Dr. Ross, "is that we can satisfy the patient's needs and not our needs. The only hope we can give very sick children of a very young age is to allow parents—I don't say mothers—I mean parents, to be with small children as often and as long as necessary."

137

Not only does such a procedure offer comfort to the child, but it allows parents to come to grips with the serious illness of their children.

To be sure, discussions with children of their fatal diseases can be a difficult ordeal for parents. Certainly, whether or not such discussions should take place is an individual matter. Communications between parents, clergymen, and physicians should be open. When a child asks a question it should be answered in a way he can understand. Dr. Stanford Friedman of the University of Rochester, suggests that when a child asks, "What do I have?" he may really be trying to find out whether doctors and parents are available and in control of the situation.

"A simple explanation, such as you are having trouble with your blood, may suffice with the younger child, but then he should be assured that medicine is available when he is uncomfortable, that his parents can easily reach the doctor, and that his problem is understood and being treated," Dr. Friedman says.

When a child is terminally ill the emotional strain on the family is great. The family may go through the same five stages that a dying adult does—denial, anger, bargaining, depression and grief, and acceptance. One father, for example, bargained that if his infant son could recover from a serious disease, he (the father) would strictly follow the principles of his religion for the rest of his life. In this fortunate case the child recovered, and the father became a religious man.

Experts believe that, with help, a dying adult can pass fairly quickly through the early stages and reach acceptance at an appropriate time. But when the patient is a child, and it is the family that is going through the stages, family members rarely reach the stage of acceptance before the child dies.

"Blessed are those who mourn:
for they shall be comforted."
Matthew 5:4

———◆———

7

GRIEF AND BEREAVEMENT

Just as each person must at some time face his own death, so too must he be exposed to the death of a loved one. Whether the loved one is parent, sibling, spouse, or child, the closest surviving relatives face perhaps the most trying emotional experiences in their lives. The bereaved encounter a host of emotions, many of which are bewildering. In their sorrow the bereaved are suitable targets for money-making schemes that revolve around the recent loss. One outstanding example of this in our society is the funeral and its commercial aspects. As Jessica Mitford has so ably described in the *American Way of Death,* the funeral trade is geared to extract far too much money from the bereaved. Expensive caskets, burial plots, memorials, embalming, clothing, and cosmetics for the deceased may cost a survivor a thousand or more dollars—which in a time of exaggerated emotion he gladly spends, even if he cannot afford it.

Some sort of funeral is an important rite of passage, and in every culture people surround burial with ritual. Archaeologist Chester Chard has noted that "The reason we know so much more about Neanderthaloid Man himself as compared with earlier forms is that he was the first (so far as we know) to dispose of his dead, perhaps the most striking evidence of his increasing humanity." The evolution of man has been measured in part by the way in which he disposes of his dead.

The funeral is thought to serve three general purposes: disposal of the body, aid to the survivors in reorienting themselves after the shock of a loved one's death, and a public acknowledgement of the death.

Culture and religious beliefs dictate to a large degree the mode in which disposal of the dead will be accomplished. The primary purpose of many of the traditional funeral rites—from ancient times to the present—has consistently been to offer solace and a period of healing to survivors. Modern psychiatry and psychology have acknowledged the therapeutic value of these ritual funerary ceremonies.

In Judaism, for example, the activities of the mourner follow a prescribed pattern. Since the bereaved must not weep too long or too severely for the dead, the Talmud—the body of Jewish law—limits mourning to three days for weeping, seven for lamenting, and thirty for abstaining from haircuts and the wearing of pressed clothes.

Jewish ritual also provides for companionship for the bereaved. According to one ancient tradition, mourners are forbidden to eat of their own bread on the funeral day. This necessitated that others visit the home to bring food; presumably they also offered comfort and compassion.

The sitting of *shivah* lasts for seven days, during which the mourner sits on a low stool and receives consolation from friends and relatives. For eleven months following the death of a parent the bereaved recites a special prayer, the *Kaddish,* daily. After the first eleven months, however, *Kaddish* is recited only on the anniversary of the death. Again, this custom prescribes significant mourning (i.e., at least a daily prayer) for a set length of time, and prohibits excessive grief (at least in this way) thereafter. Interestingly, although the *Kaddish* is known as the prayer of the dead it does not once mention the dead or death. Rather it is a prayer summoning all to acknowledge God as the creator and ruler of the world and expressing hope that during the lifetimes of those listening, the Kingdom of God will be established on earth. The *Kaddish,* states Rabbi Simon Greenberg of the Jewish Theological Seminary, in New York, "is a humble and faithful acceptance of God's decree."

In a study by Robert Fulton and Gilbert Geis it was found that American rabbis, whether Orthodox, Conservative, or Reform, tend to see the "purpose of the funeral ceremony in much the same light. For them, the funeral is basically a religious service which not only serves to honor God, but which pays tribute to the deceased. It is a ceremony which assuages the grief of the survivors and is a comfort to them in their loss. The funeral also is seen to be educational, i.e., to arouse thought about a better life."

Another traditional funeral custom is the wake. Literally the word means "to watch a corpse." The custom is of unknown origin, although according to sociologist Jerome Salomone, "waking the dead almost certainly was invented before the advent of civilization and is found all over the world."

Formerly waking was an uninterrupted watch of the dead body from the time of death until burial. Most familiar, of course, is the Irish wake, where family and friends gathered to view the corpse and to engage in eating and drinking. The custom of the wake still exists in many societies today, as a specific period when the dead person is exposed for public viewing before burial.

John J. Kane, professor of sociology at Notre Dame University explains the functions of the wake in this way: "The various preparations required for a wake undoubtedly kept the bereaved busy. And while they were certainly sad, the visitation by large numbers of friends and relatives, who were paying their last respects to the deceased, did offer some comfort. . . . Despite its aspects of merriment, even excessive drinking and brawling, the wake was still intended to be a reverent matter."

One widow, discussing her husband's wake, said it helped her because, "I saw him at home and in the hospital, suffering and in pain. When I saw him in the funeral home it made me feel much better because he was fixed up so nice and he looked so good."

Calling hours and visitations hold similar significance. It

is during these times that each religion prescribes that individuals pay their respects, not only to the dead but to the living.

The modern shift toward funerals in which much of the ceremony is dispensed with in favor of a more personal service can be considered an extension of some of the most profound traditions. Participants in such funerals explain that they seem to be more concerned with humanity than show.

Although arrangements for burial and the funeral itself may be a profound emotional experience for the bereaved, the most difficult period of adjustment takes place in the weeks and months that follow. Few individuals are aware of the deep, often conflicting feelings they may expect to experience, or the psychological and physiological symptoms that are likely to accompany grief.

Questions regarding the many aspects of grief are frequently asked of physicians, counselors, and clergymen. It is not unusual for friends and relatives to express alarm that a recently bereaved person has "gone to pieces" when he is merely experiencing normal grief. This chapter will be devoted to a discussion of some of the manifestations of normal as well as pathological grief. Perhaps the best way to begin such a discussion is to note that human beings are not alone in the animal kingdom in experiencing a special grief behavior. It has been observed, for example, in monkeys and apes. The female gorilla or rhesus monkey, following the death of her infant, is likely to carry the body around with her for days as if she were denying the fact of the baby's death. Mourning behavior in geese has been described by biologist Konrad Lorenz. Parallel this brief description with known mourning behavior in humans and the similarities are remarkable. "The first response to the disappearance of the partner consists of the anxious attempts to find him again. . . . [The goose] loses all courage and flees even from the youngest and weakest geese. . . . The lonely goose rapidly sinks to the lowest step in the ranking order. . . . The goose can become extremely shy, reluctant to approach human beings and to come to the feeding place; the bird also develops a tendency to panic. . . . Geese, after having lost their partners, took up again their long neglected connection with parents and siblings."

Some experts describe normal grief as an illness, but others dismiss this concept, citing the fact that grief is actually "normal" and self-limiting in the majority of cases. In 1917, Sigmund Freud observed that "although grief involves grave departures from the normal attitude to life, it never occurs to us to regard it as a morbid condition and hand the mourner over to medical treatment. We rest assured that after a lapse of time it will be overcome and we look upon any interference with it as inadvisable and even harmful."

Twentieth-century society's attitudes toward death and dying may indeed have complicated the process of grieving, since we tend to urge the repression of grief. Giving in to grief is considered by many to be degrading, morbid, or unhealthy. Thus friends and relatives often feel the need to distract the bereaved with diversions to help "take them out of themselves," or get away from the tragedy. Discussion about whether mourning behavior is to be considered an illness or not is really moot, an exercise in semantics. At the lowest common denominator, grief and bereavement can be described as a period in which an individual or family unit is under severe emotional and psychological strain due to the loss of a loved one.

Physicians throughout the ages have suspected that grief is a significant cause of sickness and death. This hypothesis has been borne out in studies which have confirmed exceptionally high rates of morbidity and mortality among bereaved adults of all ages.

Such studies lend statistical significance to the possibility that it may not be uncommon for the bereaved to actually die of a "broken heart." In 1967, Dr. W. Dewi Rees, a general practitioner from Llanidloes, Wales, and Sylvia Lutkins, his statistician colleague, began studying close relatives of 371 residents of Llanidloes who died over a six-year period. In the *British Medical Journal* they reported their evidence which statistically confirmed the existence of something that could be called a "broken heart syndrome." During the first year of bereavement, they found, nearly 5 per cent of the group who lost a close relative also died, while in a control group the death rate was less than 1 per cent. Even more striking, the death rate among widowers and widows was 12 per cent during the first year after the death of a spouse, while only 1.2 per cent of their counterparts in the control group died. More widowers (19.6 per cent) than widows (8.5 per cent) died. If a spouse or child died suddenly outside of the home or hospital, the death rate of survivors went up by a factor of five, a phenomenon attributable, perhaps, to the sudden shock of the death.

Why do the bereaved die more frequently than their counterparts who have not lost loved ones? Dr. Rees believes that the emotional stress of the loss of a near one may lower the body's resistance to disease and even affect a person's "will to live." This hypothesis is confirmed by others, including Dr. George Engel, a psychiatrist at the Rochester School of Medicine, who has studied the psychological causes of illness for more than twenty years. "Our theory," says Dr. Engel, "is that there is a psychological state called the 'giving up-given up' complex. A person in this state feels unable to cope with the situation, and then feels helpless or hopeless. If he is a candidate for diabetes [for example] then the disease may appear at this time of stress."

The evidence that more widowers than widows die during bereavement may be attributable to the amount of emotional stress that is built up in the individual. While women are expected to, and do, freely express their emotions, men are often expected to supress them. "Men don't cry," they are encouraged to keep a "stiff upper lip."

Among bereaved individuals, studies show that such symptoms as insomnia, trembling, nightmares, general nervousness, and depression occur with considerably more frequency than in control groups. In addition, psychosomatic symptoms such as headache, vomiting, indigestion, excessive appetite, loss of appetite, chest pain, frequent infection, and general aching are also more prevalent in the bereaved.

Sometimes a bereaved person may suffer from symptoms similar to those that caused the death of his relative. The mechanism that causes such physiological manifestations of grief is not fully understood. Specialists do point out, however, that many of the physical complications of grief might be avoided, or effectively controlled, if doctors were more aware of recent or anticipated losses that could effect their patients. Patients, of course, must be willing to communicate. Many physicians believe that by encouraging a close doctor-patient relationship during the periods of greatest stress, the bereaved could be helped to work through his normal grief so it does not become a source of lasting physical or mental incapacity.

At New York's Montefiore Hospital, Dr. Alfred Weiner and his colleagues have studied a group of bereaved individuals and the physical, emotional, and social difficulties they encountered during the first year after the death of a loved one. "We believe," the psychiatrist explains, "that one of the major problems with bereavement is a lack of social involvement with another human being, and there is some evidence from the psychiatric literature that the problems of bereavement are due to unresolved guilt."

The process of grief is one that all adults experience at one time or another in their lives. To be sure, this response to the "psychic wound" inflicted by death is statistically normal, but a producer of pain and suffering nevertheless. Most individuals are able to accept and carry out their grief work in a relatively comfortable way. Others do not resolve their grief, and thus delay or repress it. This is no solution, however, since the grief will one day surface as an entity in itself or manifest itself in abnormal behavior. The basic task of grief and mourning is the giving up of relationships with the dead loved one and then redirecting energies toward the establishment of new ties. This is best aided by encouraging the bereaved to express his feelings, which may include yearning, anger, fear, depression, panic, helplessness, hopelessness, or emptiness. Those individuals who cannot recognize and express their feelings and emotions, says Dr. Weiner, "are the ones that run into difficulties whether they be emotional, medical, or social."

Dr. Weiner and his colleagues have been instrumental in inaugurating a program whereby professional counselors, generally psychiatric nurses or psychiatric social workers, help the bereaved work through the grieving process. This program, at Montefiore Hospital in the Bronx, New York, is an involuntary one, that is, the help is generally not solicited by the bereaved. The family physician of a newly bereaved patient usually alerts a member of the program and indicates the need for help, after which a counselor telephones the family or individual to explain the program. Help is offered in all areas, including legal aid if needed.

Some of the prospective clients say they are not interested, in which case the persistent staff member will call several times. If a person is reticent to talk, the counselor tries to verbalize what is involved for him. In general, this approach has been successful. One counselor noted that of some eighty families she contacted, there were only three who would not accept help in any form. Nevertheless there were many who were afraid to accept the help, afraid to express their need. "They try to convey to you the fact that they are terribly independent, they don't need any help," the counselor explains. "But when we call them we find they don't hang up on us. The more we talk the more they allow themselves to open up, even the most independent ones. People have to be educated to begin with to the idea of such a service. It is very difficult for people to accept psychiatric help in general."

Another program, focusing on widows, exists at the Harvard Medical School's Laboratory of Community Psychiatry under the direction of Phyllis R. Silverman. Called the "Widow-to-Widow" program it was developed "as a result of finding in a pilot study that most people do not get close to someone in mourning, that the assistance they do offer is superficial and full of platitudes, and without real comprehension of what is needed to successfully cope and make the needed changes to build a new life."

In the Harvard program the clients are all newly bereaved women under sixty in the Boston area. The "care givers," as the name of the program implies, are other widows who live in or near the community, but are strangers to the women they visit. As widows themselves the care-givers, whose religious and racial backgrounds are matched to their clients, can give relevant insight to the women they contact.

Initial contacts are made by telephone, and telephone

146

"visits" may be continued as often as desired by the client. Eventually most of the clients and care-givers meet in person. Results have been gratifying and about 60 per cent of the widows offered help accepted. The women who refuse "claim to be involved with family as helpers and are less ready to accept an outsider as a potentially helping person. Also, they seem to be eager to project an adequate, self-sufficient image of themselves," Dr. Silverman says.

One interesting aspect of both the Harvard and Montefiore programs is that the bereaved person does not have to seek out help. This is the way it should be according to Dr. Silverman, who notes that "the nature of bereavement is such that the grieving person finds it very difficult to ask for help, let alone find the energy to seek out a resource in the first place."

This is only one aspect of behavior that the bereaved must cope with. Normal grief may take a number of forms and it is important for individuals to be able to recognize these in themselves and their friends and relatives, for, while doctors and psychiatrists with their armory of chemicals and diagnostic equipment can often be of help, the most positive therapy emanates from a close circle of understanding friends and relatives. "If sorrow works," said Macbeth, "the grief that does not speed knits up the overwrought heart and sets it free."

In a study of widows, psychiatrist C. Murray Parkes of the Tavistock Institute of Human Relations in London found that the women passed through three successive, but overlapping, stages of grief. The first stage is numbness, lasting from a few hours to a few days after the husband's death. One widow described this feeling as "like walking on the edge of a black pit." The woman added that she "felt nothing at all" when first told of her husband's death. She consciously avoided her feelings for fear she would be overcome by them and go insane.

The second and most acute stage of grief was yearning and protest. The women cried and directed their attentions to places and things they associated with their dead husbands. Many described perceptual illusions in which they saw or heard him. "In my dream," one widow said, "he was in the coffin with the lid off and all of a sudden he came to life and got out. I looked at him and he opened his mouth. I said, "He's alive. Thank God. I'll have him to talk to.' "

Dr. Parkes also reported that the widows frequently would identify with a dead spouse in any number of ways, including behaving or thinking as he would, developing physical symptoms similar to those of his terminal illness, and feeling that the dead husband was actually "inside me" or present in their children. During the most intense times of the second stage of grief all the widows suffered from insomnia and loss of appetite. The emotional distress of the widows was never continuous, however, and it was followed by periods of relative calm. To achieve these, a number of defense mechanisms including denial, disbelief, forgetting selectively, or pleasant fantasies about the husband, were used.

The third stage of grief consisted of feelings of apathy, aimlessness, and disorganization, coupled with "a disinclination to look to the future or see any purpose in life." Nearly two thirds of the widows that Dr. Parkes studied were still experiencing these symptoms after the first year of bereavement.

Robert Anderson wrote, as the first and last lines of his play *I Never Sang for My Father,* "Death ends a life, but it does not end a relationship, which struggles on in the survivor's mind towards some resolution which it never finds."

Indeed the bereaved has lost a part of himself or herself. Many express their feelings of loss in just that way. "I feel as if a part of me is gone." The bereaved individual feels numbness. There is great difficulty in accepting the reality of the situation. What can be called "panic attacks" may arise in the first few days after the death. The attacks may consist of anxiety, palpitations, sweating, pining for the lost one, a tightness in the throat, and copious tears. It is a restless time, this first week. Then and afterward the individual may face the consequences of what psychiatrists call separation anxiety, a form of search for the lost object. Again, this is a period of pining and yearning for the lost person, just as Dr. Parkes found in his study of widows.

A survey of the psychiatric literature pertaining to grief shows a fairly general consensus that normal mourning is made up of three phases. First is a short period of shock, second a period of intense grief, and finally a period of recovery and the resumption of normal social life.

In older persons the grief reaction is sometimes far less intense than in younger individuals. It is speculated that this may be due to the fact that older persons have primed themselves for a particular loss, or perhaps have suffered so many previous losses that they become almost immune to the final loss. Their children have left home, they have retired, their parents and peers have died; all of these are losses.

Older persons often expect the death of the spouse or their peers, just as younger persons often anticipate death in their older relatives. "Grief reactions," says Dr. Samuel Lehrman, "are actually much more normal when death occurs in an aged person and has been expected. Under such circumstances, the work of mourning is done quickly, because a certain amount of this work . . . has already preceded the event of death."

This is called anticipatory or preparatory grief, a situation in which an individual may actually begin to grieve the loss of a loved one before he has died. This may occur when a person learns a loved one is terminally ill, or entering the final phase of a long illness. When anticipatory grief has occurred, the shock phase of grief is often eliminated because preparations have already been made, sympathies expressed, and grief experienced before death. It is gradually replaced by acceptance of the situation. Although sharp grief was already experienced when the outcome became obvious, an acute stage of grief still comes at the time of death.

In counseling the bereaved, Mrs. Delia Battin, chief social worker of Montefiore Hospital's bereavement project, explains, "We try to encourage them to talk about all kinds of details from their lives starting with courtship, marriage, family events to cover the entire relationship through life with the departed." The good as well as the bad must be discussed, for guilt is a common problem with the bereaved. It may be guilt stemming from a recent argument with the deceased, or a long-standing feud. The survivor may be tormented with thoughts of what might have been done for the departed during his final days. "I should have called the doctor two days earlier," is a typical response. A spouse or parent may also feel guilt-ridden for no other reason than that he has survived.

Guilt may also be a result of anger toward the deceased. "I knew she couldn't control the fact that she was dying," one young husband said, "but sometimes I was mad at her for leaving me and our daughter." Anger is another universal component of grief. A person may be angry at the world for going on as usual after his loved one has died. He may be angry at the deceased for having left him alone, or at the doctor for "killing" the loved one, or not doing all that was medically possible. One family, upset at the death of an elderly aunt, vented anger at their physician for "not keeping her alive until she got to be one hundred." God or the clergyman may also be targets for anger since they "allowed this to happen."

Those dealing with bereaved persons, should be prepared for such anger reactions, and understand their significance. The verbal target is not the actual target of wrath, and emotional outbursts of anger or accusation on the part of the bereaved only reflect a tremendous frustration because of their own inability to prevent the death.

Although such situations may prove difficult, the anger should not be suppressed, but encouraged and discussed. The bereaved may be patiently and gently assured that he, and the doctors, did everything they could in caring for the deceased. This may help absolve the person of some of his self-inflicted guilt.

In addition to anger, the bereaved experiences fears of loneliness and abandonment. Loneliness can be terribly frightening, especially to one who has lived with a person for many years and then loses him. Relatives should be encouraged to be available as often as possible—not only for the customary first few days or weeks after the death, but for many months. Loneliness can be allayed to a great degree by helping the bereaved person to feel needed. A young woman, for example, who has lost her father and asks her mother to do something as simple as baby sitting, can offer her a meaningful and therapeutic experience.

As has already been noted, the grieving person finds it difficult to ask for help. Therefore friends and relatives who say "Call if you need me," or "I'll do anything, just let me know," aren't really offering assistance. Concrete suggestions—an invitation to dinner or an outing—or small gifts of food or other things the bereaved is known to like would certainly be welcome. Help in these more tangible forms is not likely to be refused, and graphically expresses the sympathy and care of the giver. Ideally, special consideration of the bereaved should continue over a period of months. Many bereaved individuals need this extra help and support after a loved one has died.

Unfortunately it is not uncommon for friends and relatives of bereaved individuals to withdraw from them, just as they may have from the dying person. Friends or relatives feel uncomfortable with the anxiety, pain, and sadness of grief, and do not know how to handle their own anxieties. Embarrassed about what to say, they resort to excuses such as "We don't want to talk about it because we'll upset Auntie."

Excuses or not, according to Dr. Weiner, "That's a lot of baloney. The best thing you can do for a bereaved person is to talk about the dead person." The bereaved can then review the experiences shared with the deceased. Talking out the situation helps the individual experience his loss. Friends and relatives often fear that the bereaved will cry or become visibly upset. In fact, this is exactly what is needed, because it is only by turning grief outward that a person can once again resume normal living. At the same time, it is possible for a friend or relative to encourage too much discussion. The bereaved may indicate that there has been enough talk for a time. If this happens, an understanding person should recognize that what the bereaved may really need is simply the comforting presence of someone who cares.

Detailed discussions of the many emotional states a bereaved person goes through will also help him cope with his need to deny the death. It is not uncommon for recently bereaved persons to think, say, and partially believe statements like, "It's not really true," "It's a dream," or "She is really away on a trip." One woman set the dinner table for two every evening for six months after her husband's death, expecting him to come home. Other people

151

experience hallucinations and delusions that seem quite real. There is a preoccupation with thoughts of the deceased. Attention is directed to places and objects associated with the lost person. The bereaved may often visit the hospital where the loved one died or the cemetery where he or she is buried. Many people have great difficulty disposing of the clothing of the deceased for the first three to six months. For some, nothing in the home must be changed. Pictures must be displayed, pipes and slippers must remain, ties must hang in the same place, and so forth.

Mrs. J., whose husband had just died, would "see" her husband every evening at six o'clock on his deathbed. At first she was alarmed by the experience. After talking with her counselor—a social worker from the Montefiore program—however, it became clear that this was the time when Mrs. J. was most lonely. It was the time her husband would have come home from work for dinner. The woman needed to see her husband, so she did. Even though she saw him on his deathbed, he was still alive and present. It was a positive experience for the woman. As her grief subsided she gradually gave up the hallucination.

Other bereaved individuals may hear familiar sounds; the key in the front door, the garage door going up, somebody walking around upstairs. A bereaved person may look out the window and see someone walking in the street who resembles (in mind at least) the spouse. They may say to themselves, or even aloud, "Ah, yes, he's coming home." And for a moment they actually believe it to be true.

For the first few weeks after his wife's death, one fifty-seven-year-old man felt as if she were lying next to him in bed every night. He smelled her, he felt her, he heard her. In his mind, she was there.

"This is not crazy," says Dr. Weiner. "This is all normal. People think, 'Am I going crazy?' and the answer, simply, is 'No, you are not going crazy. This is mourning.'"

If all of these behavioral states ranging from loneliness to hallucinations and physical symptoms are normal manifestations of grief, then how is a person to know when his (or another's) grief reaches a point of pathology, serious disturbance?

This is a difficult question to answer specifically, of course, because the range of normality differs in each case. One signal of abnormal grief, according to Mrs. Delia Battin, is when people don't cry. "That is abnormal. I'm also suspicious of people who act as if nothing at all has happened." In other words one of the most common indications of pathology of grief is the absence of visible grief. Dr. Weiner adds that "Grief becomes abnormal when it interferes with social functions for an extended period. When a person never goes out, can't work, or if drinking or a similar problem arises."

In normal grief it is common for the individual not to sleep for days or even weeks, to have a poor appetite initially and then to overeat. It is even normal to have suicidal thoughts.

"People get very scared about suicidal talk," says Mrs. Battin, "but it is normal. I have seen it a great deal. I too would have been frightened at the beginning, hearing that someone wants to turn on the gas and die, but I find now that these are really normal feelings and it is important to help the bereaved to express them." Psychiatrists have pointed out that most individuals who talk about or attempt suicide don't really want to die. What they do want is more attention, love, understanding, and companionship. Nevertheless, if a bereaved individual begins talking a great deal about suicide, it is wise to seek professional help immediately.

In her extensive therapeutic interviews with nearly one hundred bereaved individuals and families, Mrs. Battin has also noted a heightened suspicious attitude. "Again, this seems to be normal, and again, it makes sense because when a person gets hurt he can become oversensitive. This acute sensitivity makes for a perception of details in other people's behavior and attitudes, which take on 'unfriendly' shades and meanings, and this can result in a certain suspicious attitude. Naturally there are all kinds and degrees and if a person becomes openly and obviously paranoid, then we can talk about pathology."

The rare possibility of paranoid delusion in the bereaved is seen in the case of a sixty-four-year-old housewife whose husband died after heart surgery. The woman had never gotten along well with her husband. They had been separated several times and serious arguments were common in their marriage. After the man's death, his widow withdrew and became increasingly suspicious of neighbors and friends. She began to accuse the doctor and hospital of having killed her husband. Through a lawyer she began malpractice proceedings against the surgeon and hospital. As the attorney became aware of her paranoid state, however, he persuaded her against further proceedings. With the lawyer's help, the woman contacted a psychiatrist who treated her with medication and supportive psychotherapy. Gradually she reviewed her marriage in detail, mourned the loss of her husband, and was able to reach a more normal attitude.

The question of how long normal grief and bereavement should last is a perplexing one, mainly because the answer is vague. In the past, the psychiatric literature has described this period as lasting between three and six months. More recently, however, physicians have become less concerned with actual time limits. They have found the three-to-six-month rule not to be true. "We find that grieving can continue for a year, two years, or even longer. And to some extent it is never resolved," Dr. Weiner says.

In his book *Dying*, Dr. John Hinton notes that to define any period of grief as unduly long implies that "there is a generally accepted length of mourning. In fact the duration of sorrow varies enormously. Usually, the more severe mental pain eases after one or two or perhaps a few more weeks. . . . In psychiatric practice and life in general, it is far from rare to meet people whose depression smoulders on and on after their bereavement, blighting their lives for years."

Thus it is the progress of the course of grief that is the overriding factor, and not necessarily the length of time it takes. Generally this progress can be judged by how well the bereaved undertakes a gradual return to the level of functioning he had attained before the loss. The formation of new relationships, and the return to a capacity for pleasure without guilt or shame are also indications of recovery from bereavement. It should be expected, however, that a bereaved individual will experience upsurges in grief when faced with special events such as anniversaries, or objects reminding him of the deceased. This may occur months or years after the loss.

Many individuals, when first faced with grief, will approach their physicians for medications. "I know I won't be able to sleep or eat, doctor, won't you give me something?" Some doctors acquiesce, with no further questions asked, but the indiscriminate treatment of bereaved individuals with various kinds of mood-altering drugs has become somewhat controversial. Many specialists no longer accept this mode of therapy except in rare cases, although the use of mild sedation is still, and probably will remain, common.

"I do not believe that in the vast majority of cases [the use of mood-changing drugs] is indicated," says Dr. Weiner, who adds, "I believe that the best tranquilizer, or the best mood elevator, is to have another human being. I do not believe that most of the emotional problems following bereavement are of such severity that they require medication. It's almost like taking a sledgehammer to kill a fly. Unfortunately too many people do this. In this particular culture at this moment you have a little ache, you take a drug or something."

It is true, after all, that an individual can face a crisis in more than one way. He can succumb to it physically or emotionally, or he can grow through having suffered. Perhaps by overprescribing medications to the bereaved, physicians are doing them a disservice. It is accepted that some suffering, with proper support and guidance, can indeed be therapeutic. Since grief has a natural course, many psychiatrists feel there is little reason to use mood-altering medication for normal mourning.

"Normal grief work," says Dr. A. H. Schmale of the University of Rochester Medical Center, "cannot be delayed or changed in any major way by such external factors as drugs."

Certainly if the patient's suffering is intense and there is severe depression and he cannot sleep, most would agree that a medication may be indicated for use over a specified period of time. Nevertheless such drugs as tranquilizers and stimulants and antidepressants must be prescribed carefully and used selectively. The greatest danger of chemotherapy during bereavement, physicians point out, is that it is too easy for a doctor to say, "Here are your pills, goodbye," and not provide the most important of all therapies, understanding.

"death, thou shalt die!"
John Donne, "Death Be Not Proud"

———————◆———————

DEATH AND THE DEEP FREEZE

On Sunday, July 28, 1968, twenty-four-year-old Steven Jay Mandell was declared dead at Manhattan's Columbia Presbyterian Hospital. Cause of death: chronic intestinal inflammation and complications.

The young man was dead, but he was not to be buried. Nor was he to be cremated. His body would not turn to dust; his organs would not be used for transplantation. Instead he would become the seventh American to take a chance—however remote—of being brought back to life in the future.

Seven months before he died, Mandell, who had been ill for some time, joined the Cryonics Society of New York, which advocates freezing human bodies at death in the hope that someday they can be thawed back to life when science can cure the fatal illness. The student decided that he would take a long-shot on his own possible resurrection. So Steven Jay Mandell, a New York University aeronautical engineering student, was frozen.

Shortly after he was pronounced dead by a hospital physician the Cryonics Society of New York (CSNY) was

157

notified by Mandell's aunt that the student had died. "Since Mr. Mandell, a member of the Society, had been insured with the Aetna Insurance Co. for $10,000 payable to his mother upon death, we decided to take immediate action," CSNY records state.

Frederick Horn, director of the St. James, Long Island, Funeral Home drove to the city to claim the body and transport it to his facilities. Other members of the society's cryonic suspension team were informed. They gathered materials and equipment necessary to administer the treatment and met at the white frame building in the tiny Long Island town where Horn officiates over some fifty conventional funerals yearly.

Mandell's body was kept under refrigeration in the hospital morgue until Horn arrived. He packed the body in ice for the hour-plus drive to St. James. Early Sunday afternoon the body was brought into Horn's embalming room, lifted onto an embalming table, and treatment was initiated. White uniform-clad CSNY members, like a special squad from the land of science fiction, applied ice packs to the body. Horn injected the patient's blood vessels with a protective chemical solution which would hopefully minimize freezing damage to cells. Using a mechanical heart pump adjusted to normal blood pressure, a mixture of glycerol and Ringer's solution was gradually circulated throughout the body by injection into the common carotid artery of Mandell's neck. Blood was drained from the adjacent jugular vein in the process that filled the student's body with a kind of human antifreeze solution.

After perfusion was completed, Mandell's body was cooled in a plastic bag filled with ice. After several hours it was transferred into a temporary styrofoam-insulated box packed with dry ice.

The next day, Monday, a funeral service was held for Mandell at the funeral home. About forty-five friends and relatives attended and watched as the dry-ice cooled body, in its styrofoam container, was placed in a casket and wheeled into the chapel.

The funeral director recalls, "When the rabbi gave the service he noticed that there wasn't a tear shed in the chapel and he said from the pulpit that this was the first

158

time he had ever seen such a reaction from the family and friends. "There is no grief here,' he said."

The next day, as she sat in the awkward stillness of the funeral parlor, Mrs. Pauline Mandell, Steven's mother, said, "I think there's so much less of a feeling of loss than in the normal situation, especially where there is a flicker of hope. I think my rabbi expressed it best—there is a light at the end of a long, dark tunnel."

Mrs. Mandell said that she and her son had discussed the frozen death several times and she did not resist it. "My son had a great vision of what science would do in the future and he wanted to be part of it. He had a great belief in the future of science, and if there is even the slightest chance that it might help him or someone else, then we have nothing to lose and everything to gain."

About a month later Steven Mandell's body was placed in a ten-foot-long capsule of liquid nitrogen, 321 degrees below zero Fahrenheit, at Washington Memorial Park Cemetery at Coram, New York. The $4,000 tube-shaped capsule, similar to a thermos bottle in construction, needs to be replenished regularly with liquid nitrogen to keep the temperature at the proper level. Cryonics Society officials thus service the capsule regularly, but members of the general public are not allowed to view the capsules.

Neither the practice of cooling for preservation of tissues, nor preservation of the body toward immortality is new. Though man is mortal he has long sought, and continues to seek, immortality. Some men have sought immortality of body, others immortality of soul, some have sought both.

Modern man is fascinated by Egyptian mummies; he flocks to museums to see them. The fascination with these ancient objects in many ways symbolizes man's ever-present desire to live forever.

The word *mummy* probably originated with the Arabic word for pitch, or asphalt, *mumiya,* which was one of the many substances the Egyptians used to embalm their dead. The similarity between the two words led to a bizarre European medical practice. Pitch was ground into an ointment for wounds and burns; often it was mixed into a potion and drunk. The pitch used supposedly came from

Egyptian tombs, and eventually medicines said to be made from ground-up bits of mummies were used. Some mummy medications were in use as recently as the last century. It is safe to say, however, that medically speaking they were of little or no value.

The ancient Egyptians would have been shocked at this disrespect for the carefully preserved bodies. They believed in a soul, or *ka,* distinct from the body. But they linked the immortality of the *ka* to survival of the body itself, thus their emphasis on the elaborate ritual of corpse preservation.

Other civilizations practiced similar corpse preservation techniques. To a large extent Inca society was organized around the concept that their rulers did not really die and would return someday to rule again. Thus the mummy of a dead ruler was set up in one of the villas and was treated as if it were alive; flies were whisked away, meals were served, family members came to consult with the dead man and he answered them—through a specially appointed oracle. At important state occasions all of the dead kings were gathered together for special ceremonies at the Inca capital. The deeds of each of the kings were recalled in song and dance, and the dead kings toasted each other through their descendants.

When the Inca empire fell to the Spanish in 1533, the royal Inca line could be traced back through nine kings. It seems unlikely that the society could have continued much longer, for the cost of maintaining large households for nine dead men was already a large burden.

Some mummies are associated with our own culture. Jeremy Bentham, the British philosopher who died in 1832, believed that preserved skeletons could serve posterity. Thus, when Bentham died, his body was dissected and the skeleton reconstructed. The bones were fitted with a molded wax head, dressed in Bentham's clothes, and seated inside a glass-fronted case at the University College in London. Bentham can be viewed there today with his real head, in a mummified state, resting between his skeleton feet.

Benjamin Franklin speculated upon the possibility of being embalmed in such a way to preserve the body so as to allow reanimation at some future date. In a 1773 letter to Barber Dubourg he wrote, "I wish it were possible from this instance to invent a method of embalming drowned persons, in such a manner that they may be recalled to life, however distant."

Franklin's idea was embalming in wine. The "instance" he refers to, so the story goes, occurred on a summer afternoon when he sat on the patio of his home in Philadelphia discussing the weather and the time of day with friends. Franklin sent a servant to the wine cellar to fetch a bottle of Portuguese wine. Franklin opened the bottle and poured for his friends. Doing so, he noticed that a few fruit flies fell from the bottle into the glasses. One of his friends said that he had heard that the fruit flies could be brought back to life by drying them in the sun.

This was done, and it is said that three or four of the flies brushed off their wings, wriggled about, and flew away. This prompted Franklin to say something like, "On the day of my demise I would like to have myself and a couple of my friends cast into hogshead of alcohol to be stored away and struck open in future generations so I might emerge and see what they've wrought."

Actually there is evidence that people have been embalmed in liquor, although not for the purpose of recalling them to life. When a young woman named Nancy Martin died at sea in 1857, her father did not want a sea burial, so he had her body thrust into a cask of alcohol and returned to this country. The cask and contents were buried in Oaksdale Cemetery, Wilmington, North Carolina.

According to some of Lord Nelson's biographers, the admiral was returned to England from Trafalgar in a barrel of rum. Obviously the desire for preservation of body produced a number of ingenious attempts to find a satisfactory preservative.

One of these is cold. Occasionally reports have been published of prehistoric animals, or parts of them, being materially preserved in glaciers. And certainly it may be speculated that long before man deliberately preserved his food by freezing, he was somewhat aware of cold's value. What must prehistoric man have thought when, at the first thaw of spring, he came upon a dead and frozen beast whose meat was as fresh and tasty as one just killed?

Undertakers have long recognized the action of cold as

161

a preserver of the corpse. One embalming guide notes that rigor mortis, like most chemical reactions, "is accelerated by heat and retarded by cold. Complete freezing of the dead body prevents the onset of rigor mortis, but as soon as the body is thawed, rigor mortis will appear quickly and remain for only a short period of time."

Long before the invention of mechanical refrigeration units, undertakers utilized ice and cold for the storage of corpses charged to them. These funeral directors, however, apparently had no intention of using cold for long-term storage of the body—though it was effective for short-term preservation. In 1846, two Baltimore undertakers, C. A. Trump and Robert Frederick received a patent for a "Refrigerator for Corpses." Three years earlier the first "corpse preserver," based on the principles of ice refrigeration had been patented by John Good of Philadelphia.

Cooling boards and corpse coolers continued to be patented and used until the latter part of the nineteenth century, but many undertakers had become so well acquainted with ice cooling as a corpse preservation technique that they continued to use the method until early in the twentieth century.

The science of cryobiology, however, has arisen within the past few decades. Cold is used by scientists to preserve tissues and organs, as well as to destroy unwanted ones, as in cryosurgery—cutting with a scalpel which has been rendered supereffective by subzero temperatures. *Kryos* is the Greek word for "icy cold" or "frost." Cryobiology describes the relatively new science in which the effects of low temperatures on living systems are studied and used. The branch of technology that deals with the generation and maintenance of very low temperatures is called cryogenics. Cryonics, however, is, as described by one of its foremost proponents, "a blanket to cover all the disciplines and programs centered on human cold storage."

The first tissue to be stored by freezing for medical purposes was blood. In the late 1940s Dr. Basile Luyet of the Rockefeller Institute discovered that large percentages of the red cells in ox blood survived extremely low temperatures, provided freezing was carried out very rapidly. Techniques now have been developed which permit the rapid freezing of human blood so it can be kept in storage for years—with minimal damage to blood cells. Fully 80 to 85 per cent of the cells survive the quick freeze and thaw.

Whole goldfish have been frozen and thawed back to life after a short period of time by scientists, and some small mammals have been cooled near the freezing point (but not frozen solid) and survived with minimal damage.

In a paper in the British science journal *Nature,* scientists reported the successful freezing and thawing of mouse embryos in England. Japanese professors Isamu Suda, K. Kito, and C. Adachi cooled a cat's brain which had been perfused with glycerol to minus four degrees Fahrenheit and stored it for 203 days. After thawing the brain, the scientists found that the organ registered almost normal electroencephalograph (EEG) readings. The Kobe University scientists wrote that they "wish to conclude that brain cells are not especially vulnerable to lack of oxygen. It appears that even nerve cells of the brain can survive and be revived after long-term storage under special circumstances."

A question remains as to whether the EEG reading represented the cat's organized brain function—what we would refer to in humans as thought or, on a higher level, reason—or incoherent electrical activity. Nevertheless, cryonics believers see the experiment as just one more sign pointing toward the mastery of the freezer for man.

Another such sign was reported in 1972 when three Soviet scientists stated in *Nature New Biology* that they had found that "cooling after death favours not only the maintenance of the ability to restore protein biosynthesis but also the ability to resume vital activity of the animal as an integral system—the cardiac cycle, breathing, corneal reflex and sometimes motor response to stimulation begin again."

The Russians cooled dead rabbits to temperatures a few degrees above freezing. After up to an hour the rabbits were rewarmed and reanimated, at which time the scientists found that the animals' manufacture of protein was restored in all of the organs, but at very low levels in the spleen and brain. Postmortal cooling, they concluded, may

163

possibly prolong the period "between the cessation of vital activity and loss of vitality, and so . . . increase the probability of body reanimation . . . after death."

At least one insect, the carpenter ant of North America, has already solved cryonic suspension for itself. Each year as winter approaches, the insect manufactures and saturates its tissues with an oily substance called glycerol. The compound is a good freeze-preservative, and though the ant freezes solid throughout the winter, when spring arrives he thaws and comes to life again.

Science has already succeeded in preserving human and animal semen. Once frozen, semen stored in liquid nitrogen at 321 degrees below zero Fahrenheit does not deteriorate for several years—up to ten or more according to some scientists. The Idant Corporation, which recently opened the first of a planned international chain of frozen sperm banks in New York, reports that there has been no increase in miscarriage or birth defects among the four hundred children now alive who were conceived through artificial insemination with frozen sperm. Frozen semen has been widely used for the breeding of cattle, and in 1970, some five and a half million cattle were sired in the United States by deep-freeze banked sperm. Scientists report here, too, that the rate of congenital malformation is lower than that from naturally induced pregnancies.

According to cryobiologist Dr. J. K. Sherman of the University of Arkansas School of Medicine, "The dramatic, empirically derived success in banking spermatozoa for the animal-breeding industry . . . has been economically rewarding, but with the realization of this reward, research has receded to token interest.

"Unlike banks for frozen human spermatozoa, blood, and tissue culture cells, however, human body banks have not been qualified as 'proven.' That is to say, no frozen human body from such a bank has been thawed for evaluation of the functional and structural integrity of its cells and for comparison of its condition after thawing with that at the time of freezing."

Even though the most promising method of storing viable human organs is freezing, not a single major human organ has been successfully preserved in this way. At the National Naval Medical Center, the world's pre-eminent deep-freeze bank for tissues, only three types of tissues are stored for future use: corneas, skin, and bone marrow cells.

There are no functional banks for living organs such as the heart or kidney, or for tissues of these organs. The sole reason for this is man's current ignorance of the effects of freezing as well as of the mechanisms associated with the injury caused by the possible preservation afforded by freezing, storing, and thawing of the highly complex organs or organisms.

Although no whole organs have yet been freeze-preserved, scientists have made no secret of their desires. A frozen kidney bank, for example, would be invaluable to transplant surgeons because of the vast choice of tissues available for matching. In addition, there would be no wasting of organs because of the lack of a suitable recipient at the time of a given donor's death.

The problems scientists have encountered include the fact that freezing results in the formation of ice crystals. Water to form the ice is drawn from inside cells, many of which are damaged by the microscopically beautiful, but lethal crystals. In the freezing process, then, the permeability of the cell membranes may be changed, tiny blood vessels are injured, and the electrochemical equilibrium of tissues and cells is disrupted. When frozen, the electrolyte solutions vital to life become concentrated in cells and their balance is seemingly impossible to restore upon thawing. Thus it is during the process of thawing that much of the damage to an organ or system is sustained.

However, when an organ selected for freezing is removed from an animal's body, it can be flushed out with antifreeze solutions to reduce ice crystal formation and damage. Kidneys treated this way, for example, have survived twenty-four hours of freezing, and recovered part— but not all—of their function when reimplanted in the animal from which they came. Dr. Leslie Rudolf, of the University of Virginia, has experimented with several variations of cooling and flushing with chemicals, under different pressures, to reduce cell metabolism before cooling. If methods of reducing the metabolism—or the life processes—even further can be developed, they may offer the key to preservation of a single organ. But even this comparatively simple achievement of freeze-storing a whole, living organ still lies in the distant future.

Cryonics enthusiasts, in freezing their comrades, have adopted many of the techniques of the cryobiologists. They hope that those dead, frozen today, will be sufficiently well preserved to be brought back to life by the science of the future; but even the most optimistic of them admit doubts. Funeral director Frederick Horn, who has supervised more freezings than any other person, readily admits that the circumstances surrounding the freezing of each of the already frozen thirteen individuals has been far from ideal.

He explains, "Cryonics involves doctors and doctors are quite conservative. They are trained to be conservative, and a doctor will not do anything that might reflect on his practice and reputation. Therefore he has got to move in a conservative way. We are blasting through, though. For the first time some hospitals are helping us. We are getting participation by some doctors. So it took ten, twelve, or thirteen freezings to bring this about. These thirteen persons will probably never be brought back, judging by today's standards. They will either never be brought back or be the last to be brought back for the simple reason that they were the pioneers and they didn't receive the preferential treatment that others will receive later.

"We should be all set up and right there with the dying person. As soon as the doctor cannot revive the patient the death certificate should be signed. As soon as it is signed we administer the oxygen and with the sophisticated equipment they have in hospitals today we could keep a body functioning for days. Why should a person's body ever have to suffer such irreversible damage?"

The day may come to pass, cryonics believers maintain, when the family will be able to say to the physician, "Why didn't you do this? We're holding you legally responsible for not having the machinery and equipment that you have here at the hospital available and in use in this particular case."

These are some of the facts and hopes upon which cryonics movement leader Robert C. W. Ettinger, a physics instructor at Michigan's Highland Park Community College, bases his formula for immortality. In 1947 Et-

166

tinger discovered the report of experiments carried out by French biologist Dr. Jean Rostand in which frog sperm were freeze-preserved using glycerol as an agent to prevent freezing damage. Ettinger instantly saw the possible application of this new development to preserving human lives by freezing bodies immediately after death.

For more than a decade Ettinger waited for "better qualified people" to take up the idea, but eventually he began work on his own. Ettinger's book, *Prospect of Immortality,* was privately printed in 1962, and in 1964 the volume was revised and issued by a commercial publisher. The Ettinger book is quoted chapter and verse by followers in the cryonics movement. In the book's first pages he writes:

> Most of us now living have a chance for personal, physical immortality.
>
> This remarkable proposition—which may soon become a pivot of personal and national life—is easily understood by joining one established fact to one reasonable assumption.
>
> The fact: At very low temperatures it is possible, right now, to preserve dead people with essentially no deterioration, indefinitely.
>
> The assumption: If civilization endures, medical science should eventually be able to repair almost any damage to the human body, including freezing damage and senile debility or other causes of death.

Optimistically, Ettinger adds that the arrangements for freezing and thawing will "no doubt be handled at first by individuals, then by private companies, and perhaps later by the Social Security system."

Essentially, the rationale behind the freezing of human bodies is: Mr. A. dies of a terminal disease. At the moment he is legally declared dead his body still retains biological life—practically all the cells are still alive. Arrangements already made permit freezing of the body immediately to preserve the potential viability of the bulk of these cells. Years later, a cure for his terminal disease is discovered. By this time, a means of reviving the recently deceased, as well as effective technology for thawing is

167

available. Mr. A. is thawed out, returning to his original condition. He is then restored to life, cured of his disease and rejuvenated. The man lives on until he dies of another disease or of old age; then he is again frozen and the entire cycle repeated.

Since publication of *Prospect of Immortality,* cryonic life extension societies have been founded throughout this country and the world. The slogan of the New York Cryonics Society is "Never Say Die," and their emblem is the Phoenix, classic symbol of immortality. In mythology the Phoenix is a bird that transforms itself into a new young being after five hundred years by burning itself alive so it can rise again, young and beautiful, from its own ashes.

Cryonics offers the hope of eternal life, but there are no promises or guarantees. Dr. Ettinger himself states that the proposition is based upon an assumption and a fact. The fact is merely that dead people can be preserved at very low temperatures. The assumption is that eventually medical science will be able to undo the damage that freezing has caused.

Although the "no guarantee" is implied in all of the literature of organizations and corporations dealing with cryonics, it is often lost in an avalanche of optimism. A brochure of the Cryo-Span Corporation, in Sayville, Long Island, offers "attorneys, insurance experts, estate planners, psychologists, and theologians," as well as "the full spectrum of cryonic suspension services. Its management includes the foremost proponents of the concept of life extension through cryonics."

"Life extension through cryonics," it says. Not a promise, but the statement of a tantalizing possibility. Is cryonic suspension for you? The brochure continues, "Cryonic suspension is for those unique individuals who enjoy living and believe in life. It is for those who refuse to give up the fight for survival, and who will do everything within their powers to hold off the forces of death. . . . Cryonic suspension is for those who want to be a part of the future . . . who want to contribute and to enjoy the wonders of the fantastic world of tomorrow. Cryonic suspension is for you!"

The closest the pamphlet comes to discussing what may

168

actually come to pass in the future is the offer "Postsuspension counseling [presumably for survivors] on future developments."

Cryobiologist Sherman argues, however, that "There is absolutely no scientific accomplishment associated with the freezing and storage of any living material unless the desired application of the frozen storage is demonstrated." In the case of cryonics this critical goal is the preservation of the trillions of cells which remain alive at the time the legally dead body is frozen. The success or failure of this can only be proven by completion of the cryonics cycle, and this has not been attempted. "In the absence of such demonstrated preservation by freezing," declares Sherman, "only predictions of failure can be made by those of us engaged in research in these matters."

Still, the enthusiasts sincerely believe that the science of the future will take care of them. The one thousand-plus members of cryonics societies come from all walks of life, all parts of the world. As funeral director Horn puts it, they are linked only by the concept "that damn it, you don't have to go."

Members subscribe to and avidly read newsletters such as *Cryonics Reports, Cryonics Review,* and *Immortality.* These are usually mimeographed or offset publications which report on new developments in cryonics and related research, meetings, and recent freezings. They also generally carry anecdotes reinforcing the hope and the promise of the future in their special world where the temperature approximates that of the dark side of the moon, where air freezes solid, where metals become brittle as glass, where theoretically all life processes come to a stunning halt, and where, cryonics enthusiasts believe, lies the possibility of immortality. Almost religiously the words *Cryonic Suspension* are capitalized and the word *"death"* is printed within quotation marks.

The February 1969 *Cryonics Reports,* condensed an article from a medical magazine under the headline "ALL NIGHT IN FREEZING COLD/BOY COMES BACK FROM THE 'DEAD.'"

Similar reports dot the publications and bring to mind the cults of the equally sincere—if not as theoretically plausible—miracle and faith healers.

169

An editorial in the Spring 1971 issue of *Immortality* discussed cryonics as follows:

> Cryonics confronts the problem òf death squarely and rationally, but few people are even interested in thinking about death. They prefer to ignore the problem or, if they are a bit more courageous, to approach it obliquely.
>
> The development of cryonics is essential to the space program. Astronauts on long space flights will have to be placed into suspended animation for both technical and psychological reasons. Immortality is worthless unless we wish to expand our horizons, and the exploration of the universe is one of the richest, most rewarding directions we can go in.
>
> By freezing people today we are in the process of overcoming some of the enormous technical, legal, economic, social and psychological problems that inevitably grow out of an immortality program. A successful research effort cannot be turned into a practical public program overnight. The lead time we are buying today will save many lives in the future.
>
> Cryonics is for people who enjoy and revere life. It is for people who believe they have the intelligence, imagination, and courage to shape the course of the future so that the quality of life will be enhanced.

United States cryonics societies report that many of their members have already made arrangements for their own cryonic interment. But actual freezings are few, and even though Ettinger's book was published in 1964, the first human was not deliberately placed in cryonic suspension until 1967. He was Dr. James H. Bedford, a retired psychology professor who died in Los Angeles. Dr. Bedford's capsule, originally maintained in Phoenix, Arizona, has since been replaced because of nitrogen leakage and returned to Los Angeles where it rests at an undisclosed location.

Each person expresses various reasons for the interest in cryonic suspension. Mrs. Judy Ellman, of Los Angeles, said in an interview that she was motivated toward cryonic suspension by a love for life. At the time she was suffering from an incurable bone marrow disease.

A young woman, who overrode her mother's wishes and had her father exhumed from his grave and frozen after two days in the ground, explains, "You can see the person any time you want to. Skin tone is perfectly natural. Eyebrows, eyelashes—there he is. You can go back and visit when you want to, say 'Hi'—which, to me, makes a lot more sense than going to place flowers on a Sunday afternoon on a grave, smiling benignly at the green grass, placing flowers on the rot underneath. Makes my skin crawl. Going to visit the capsule, to visit my father—my father's body (I know he's dead)—at least I see him, and I pay for perpetual care, I know it's for perpetual care to maintain his body in perfect preservation—not to maintain any trees or grass or to pay the salaries of someone to mow the grass or plant new flowers. . . . I got into this for my own peace of mind during my lifetime. Now, what happens after I die, I really don't care about. I guess, in a sense, when you freeze someone, you do, in a way, avoid the absolute cutting off that death would normally mean because you're not really cut off completely from the person.

"As to whether I believe, actually, that I will see my father walking and talking again—I can't really say that I do. I wouldn't really be amazed if it happened in my lifetime, but that wasn't the primary reason I got into it. . . . You know that's when my father will get his benefit, if he is brought back to life again; but for the present, I have my benefit . . . peace of mind . . . satisfaction."

Funeral director Frederick Horn has himself made arrangements to be placed in the deep freeze upon his death.

"This gives me a little edge here that I don't know what the future is, but I know that I have a chance to be there," Horn says. "If I don't proceed with this my chance is completely gone. I'm a curious person, maybe a downright nosy person. I would hate to miss the next couple of hundred years. And if I can do anything to capture that and if it's going to take the money that I can't take with me in the first place, then what do I have to lose?"

It costs about $20,000 to have oneself prepared, frozen, placed in a permanent cryonics storage capsule, and cared for over the years. The "caring for" entails replacement of liquid nitrogen and periodic checks of the capsule to avoid leaks. Cryonics societies suggest that those interested in cryonic suspension buy at least a $20,000 life insurance policy. Earmark $10,000 of it to purchase your capsule and have yourself frozen; the balance would go into a trust fund to be handled by your bank or attorney. (The cryonics societies have already arranged with at least one large insurance firm to supply such policies.) The maintenance cost of keeping the systems functioning correctly are about $300 a year. As the number of those frozen and stored together increases, of course, costs will go down.

With a portion of the interest from the $10,000 going toward capsule maintenance, the rest of it goes back to the principal. Thus, even in the deep freeze, "you have capital working for you for the day when medical science will bring you back."

In some instances, where the candidate for cryonic suspension has not made the proper financial arrangements, problems can arise with families who fail to make the maintenance payments. Horn cites the case of a young woman who submitted her father's body for freezing several years ago. "She's using the freezing of her father to further her career and her own little publicity gags."

The girl "spent just about enough money to have her father frozen. Now there is maintenance cost to keep up the capsule," Horn claims. "But she's not about to pay any more money. And if we don't pay it she's going to scream and holler to the newspapers that we are going to allow her father to be buried. I will never again freeze anyone unless all financial arrangements are already made."

Making the financial arrangements for one's own freezing is a relatively simple affair. But what about the financial arrangements for the rest of a person's estate? When a person is in cryonic suspension, what is his status? Are there taxes on estate earnings? Is there an estate? A will? A trust for oneself? Can a person own property if he is—at least for a time—legally dead? Would marriages survive freezing?

"It's all very confusing because there are no laws as yet," Horn explains. "At present when a person is frozen in this country he has to be dead first. So, when one is dead, the insurance company needs a death certificate. Suppose we turned over a 'suspension certificate.' They

172

wouldn't understand. They'd say that they only pay off with a death certificate, because life insurance is a death benefit. So we've got to work within the framework of the laws that we now have, and just hope to keep writing new ones to cover the future."

Of course argument of the case for or against cryonic suspension becomes moot when we consider the absolute fact that we simply do not know what the future holds.

Some still argue, however, that we should prepare for any eventualities. In reviewing *Prospect of Immortality,* the trade magazine *American Funeral Director* conceded that the book's conclusions "rest on some demonstrable scientific facts; his [Ettinger's] predictions may be within the realms of possibility. The time may come when funeral directors will prepare bodies in liquid nitrogen as a matter of routine, and cemeterians will operate 'dormantories' where 'temporarily dead' human beings will remain until some long distant moment of revival."

The magazine's executive editor Charles Kates has noted, though, that the promise of immortality, with its attendant emotional traumas would open the freezing movement "to a great deal of fraud."

As one pathologist, who asked to remain anonymous, commented, "There's money to be made in this thing. Insurance policies to be sold, capsules and maintenance. Don't believe for a minute that somebody isn't trying to start a fad to make a fast buck." Some writers have estimated the potential profit in cryonics in the trillions of dollars.

Dr. Alex Comfort, director of the famed Medical Research Council Group on Biology of Aging at London's University College regards the cryonic movement as quackery pure and simple. It could divert valuable funds from legitimate research. He views the movement as a con game with promotions designed to fit the hangups of a society that, "quite readily, finds the idea of a dying man an illiberal insult to Man."

Said Dr. Comfort in his column in *Medical Opinion* magazine,

If this is not the perfect pitch, I never saw one. Point out that anyone frozen now has as much chance of re-

173

suscitation as a flea on a double-jointed dog, even assuming that our descendants will want to revive relatives they never knew, and you challenge the Omnipotence of Technology. The spin-off benefits are equally promising: there is the blackmail angle (another grand or we defrost Auntie); the hardware angle (several thousand capsules a year at several thousand dollars each); the employment angle (thousands of live Americans earning their bread as curators of dead ancestors). Then, as a worried annuity-company executive remarked to me, "Wait until the tricksters get into it. They freeze Uncle George—he is not dead but sleeping, he can vote his stock and draw his annuity. We try to get the courts to rule that a man is dead when he appears to a reasonable person to be dead. The con-men appeal it all the way: in the end, we have to buy them off."

The cryonics society's standard argument is that a person has "nothing to lose, because you can't take it with you." Indeed you can't take the money, but would you rather gamble on being revived in one or two hundred years, or give your descendants the opportunity for a better education and a meaningful—even more comfortable—life?

In the opinion of many eminent scientists the current move to cryonic suspension is premature, fruitless, and unscientific. "The retort from the well-meaning and sincere people in the cryonics societies, that those who will their bodies to be frozen have nothing to lose, is not enough to satisfy the expense, false hopes, and disregard for scientific direction that accompany such philosophy," says one observer.

Perhaps the efforts presently expended on cryonics should be redirected toward the support of the massive amount of research that is needed if the theoretical potential of cryobiology is ever to be realized. Spinoffs from this type of research would surely offer new benefits from other aspects of the potential of low temperature in preserving or destroying living material whether in health or disease.

And what of the descendants of the cryonauts? When asked about the reactions of her family, a potential cryonics patient said, "My son said to me: 'Mom, that's too much. Do you really mean I'll have to take care of you all that time?'"

Will future generations be willing to accept the burden of bringing the frozen back to life? Even an editorial in *Cryonics Reports* has pointed out that "a pattern of placing full responsibility for the dead upon the living *cannot* be perpetuated. It is simply too expensive—physically, emotionally, and morally."

"When I am revived," Ettinger says, "I expect to be greeted by friends and relatives. I will not be thrust naked and helpless into a new world, but will be thoroughly rehabilitated by institutions devoted to this purpose, paid for by my trust funds. I will be in the company of other recent resuscitees. My education and adaptation can take as long as necessary."

Another frequent objection to cryonic suspension concerns the population problem. If nobody dies, we will someday reach a saturation point when the earth simply cannot accept more people. Will births then be banned? If this ever becomes the case, the process of evolution will come to a sudden halt. No more passing of genes and chromosomes. No more survival of the fittest, no more adaptation of the species. Will we eventually become a sterile species destined to render ourselves extinct by an overwhelming desire to live forever?

Ettinger counters that the type of person who would want to be placed in cryonic suspension is not likely to be deterred by population questions. "No one in his right mind will accept death for himself because maybe at some future time he might crowd someone."

It is interesting that little resistance to the cryonics movement has been voiced by the clergy. Perhaps they don't take it seriously. Theologians who have spoken out on the subject apparently regard the cryonics process—if indeed it is possible—as an elongation of life rather than the creation of life anew. What is the difference, they ask, between resuscitating a drowning man whose pulse has stopped and resuscitating and curing a frozen victim of disease centuries after death?

If there is indeed a difference, or whether the question will ever arise, is subject to conjecture. No one can predict the fate of Steven Jay Mandell and others who now lie suspended in a world of ice. They decided while still alive to take the miniscule chance of being restored by future science to a more healthful life than they once knew.

> "Dust thou art, and unto
> dust shalt thou return."
> *Genesis 3:19*

9

MAKE WAY FOR
THE LIVING

America's dead are neither gone nor forgotten. Stark, sprawling physical monuments to them stand in or around every city and town in the nation.

While urban areas are starved for space—especially open green space where a picnic can be enjoyed or a game of baseball can be played—it is ironic that many cities do have ample green countryside available. And it often stands exactly where it is needed most, in the middle of slums and industrial areas. But this land is dedicated to the dead instead of the living.

On the maps of planning officials cemeteries appear in stippled green—as if they were parks. The vast majority of them, however, are cold, gray wastelands which are spatially dead and all but irrelevant to the living. Entire communities lack real parks, but they have cemeteries.

Already an estimated two million acres of choice land in the United States is occupied by cemeteries. The demise of the nation's present population will further require an area equivalent to 25 per cent of Rhode Island's land mass for burial. On a municipal scale, we are talking about adding cemetery space nearly five times the acreage of Minneapolis, Minnesota, if normal burial practices are continued.

The land-use crisis is apparent. Experts confidently predict that the day will soon come when Americans will be forced into a choice between the living and the dead in distribution of open space.

The acreage of United States cemeteries in 1800 was relatively small, commensurate with the nation's population of 5.3 million. But by the year 2000 the projected population is 300 to 400 million. Even though we can expect improvements in birth control, and a decline in mortality rates, burial requirements will pose serious land problems. Urban planners can no longer minimize the significance of the open space of cemeteries. Cemetery developers can no longer randomly consign land in the urban environment to normal burial methods.

The potential of cemeteries as multipurpose space has not been aggressively pursued on a broad scale because of resistance to such innovation. But, if the country is to accommodate the living as well as the dead, changes will have to be made. Careful attention must be paid not only to future methods of interment, but to the existing cemeteries. These are becoming an increasingly critical factor in the land-use crisis since many of them are unwieldy because of age, size, condition, or other incompatibility with urban growth or renewal.

Until recently it has not even been considered that burial customs might affect the land-use considerations of cities. Sociological, economic, and religious factors have minimized conflicts between cemeteries and other land uses in urban planning.

As a federal report noted in 1970, the sanctity of burial grounds has been established legally, socially, and religiously: "In this regard, the cemetery is an open space reserve. As such, the condition, size and design of cemeteries determines their open space merit for the urban environment in which they exist. The planning consequences of maintained green spaces within urban areas are visual relief, buffering between diverse land uses, passive and active parks, and, to a considerable degree, stabilized property values. A cemetery, no matter what design form, is a potential passive green space."

The farsighted American Society of Planning Officials warned in 1950 that "If the idea of 'perpetual care' were pursued far enough we should eventually use all our land for the interment of the dead and have no land left for the living. We have already reached the point at which the distribution of land between the living and the dead is a serious problem."

In 1969, for example, Walter Thabit, a New York City planning consultant reported on land use in the Brooklyn area. In one short paragraph near the end of his sixty-two page report on land use he stated that, "No park facility is needed more in East Flatbush—or in Brownsville or East New York—than a real park with woodland at least sufficiently deep to camouflage lovers with no other alternatives for privacy than the cellars of Vandeveer Estates. This need can be met by using all or part of the eighty-nine acres of Holy Cross Cemetery."

Brooklyn's borough president at that time, Abe Stark, promptly denounced the suggestion as "insensitive, if not downright ghoulish." Stark further retorted, "Does Mr. Thabit have plans to exhume the remains of five hundred thousand people and transport them to other cemeteries? Or are the lovers, for whose privacy he so tenderly cares, expected to gambol on the graves of those we in Brooklyn hold in the deepest respect and reverence?"

The Rev. George A. Mooney, director of cemeteries for the Roman Catholic Diocese of Brooklyn, called the Thabit proposal "an affront to all men of faith who hold the remains of their loved ones in reverence."

Public support for any proposal that a cemetery be used as a park as well as a burial ground is a sensitive matter. One planner's magazine commenting on the Thabit affair said, "Success may well depend on a tactful approach that speaks cogently for multiple-use [of cemeteries] without offending the religious or social sensibilities of the public." Indeed, Thabit learned his lesson the hard way. He could, no doubt, have come up with a more purposeful illustration of possible use for his proposed cemetery-park than a haven for lovers.

The question also arises as to the possible wishes of those persons buried in the Holy Cross Cemetery—the forbears that Brooklynites hold "in deepest respect and reverence." Would those good citizens have wished upon their children, and their children's children, a lack of suitable space for recreation?

Is it possible that the surge in graveyard vandalism, especially in inner city areas, in recent years has been due to the graveyard taboo? Schoolboys who see cemeteries usurping the living space they so desperately need in fact become the vandals who upset and desecrate tombstones.

Many people, sensibly, aren't waiting for formal restoration, relandscaping, or official permission before they take advantage of the green spaces cemeteries provide. Numerous families are attracted to Woodlawn Cemetery in the Bronx, which has two hundred and fifty thousand graves on its four hundred acres. "They stroll, roll their baby carriages, walk their dogs, watch the ducks and get pleasure from the flowers," says Woodlawn president Kennerly Woody. "Our gardeners regard Woodlawn as part park, and they are very proud of it."

Similarly, in the tenements of the South Bronx, youngsters did not wait for a planning official's request before they began to use a church graveyard for recreational purposes. In 1967 children played among the stones and swung from the trees, while the Rev. Henry Moore, of St. Ann's Church told a reporter, "It's a terrible problem. It's a matter of wanting to let the children have a good playground off the streets and still wanting to preserve the beauty and history of the cemetery."

While the youngsters frolicked around the graves of Lewis Morris, a signer of the Declaration of Independence in 1776; Governor Morris, a drafter of the Federal Constitution in 1787; and the broken, dirty stones and plaques of other illustrious members of the Morris family, Rev. Moore added, "People think it's a public park. And the children think it's their turf."

"Why not?" asked the children. "It's no good in the streets, so we play here. It's the only grass in the South Bronx. You forget the difference between grass where there's people buried and other grass," said a fourteen-year-old. And another small boy added, "We know we're not supposed to play in there. Father Moore said it's holy."

What could be holier than a healthy recreation area for youngsters? Nevertheless, the church accepted a grant of $25,000 from the Morris family to repair the gravestones and build a wrought-iron fence around the cemetery.

The situation was quite the opposite in 1970 at the oldest church cemetery in New York City, where Peter Stuyvesant, many of his decendants, and other historic figures are buried. At the St. Marks Church-in-the-Bowery, brick and cobblestones were laid in arching and circular designs around dozens of flat gravestones as part of a beautification project that converted the cemetery into a stone park.

The man responsible for the project was the Rev. J. C. Allen, described as the "hippie priest," who began reclamation of the area. For years it had been littered with filth and garbage by alcoholics, delinquents, junkies, and hippies from the neighboring slums of East Greenwich Village.

More than thirty Neighborhood Youth Corps teenagers took part in the reclamation. Some of them had criminal records and others had themselves desecrated the church property and ransacked the very vaults they were now beautifying.

Explained Rev. Allen, "This is a terrible slum community, and it's blowing up. It's full of bitterness, anger, and tension and I can't ignore that or pretend it doesn't exist. In fact, I have to go out and make contact with it. These kids have been with us for years, destroying us. They're angry, tortured, and vengeful, and doing this hard, skilled work, making this playground, is probably the most productive thing they've ever done."

The circumstances that caused St. Marks to become the first church in New York to formally turn its cemetery into a playground were twofold: an attempt to combat urban deterioration and the continuing efforts of the Rev. Allen to use the church as a focal point for the revitalization of the neighborhood.

Several problems had to be overcome before the project could begin. First, an existing law forbade any change or remodeling on the exterior of a landmark building without authorization. Since Episcopal churches are autonomous

181

in their diocese, no authorization was needed from the Episcopal bishop of the city.

A severe shortage of funds was overcome with the enthusiastic support of the Landmarks Commission and a $16,000 grant from the Rockefeller Foundation. The project was launched in mid-July of 1970.

"Digging began," reported the *New York Times,* "on the site where in 1660 Peter Stuyvesant, the Governor of Nieuw Amsterdam, built a small chapel on his isolated 'bouwerie,' or farm. Here, in the middle of a forest where wolves roamed, his family, a handful of neighbors and all their slaves worshipped every Sunday."

The teenagers worked with twenty truckloads of donated cobblestones. Without disturbing the underground vaults, or covering any gravestones, they erected benches and stone mosaic pavements where the neighborhood residents now sit and play.

Still, not everyone was pleased with the project. Newspapers quoted "one successful Broadway figure (who asked not to be identified)," as saying, "It just seems odd to me. I don't think it's right for children to play on graves. I think a cemetery is sacred and I know if my relatives were there, I'd be very upset."

Others, however, were more compassionate. Hamilton Fish Armstrong, a seventh-generation descendent of Peter Stuyvesant commented, "I feel nostalgic and sentimental about this lovely old place. My grandmother is buried there in her jewels and a brown coffin, and I approve heartily of everything Allen is trying to do."

The Rev. Allen himself summed it up best when he noted that there had been a few who complained to him about the graveyard project. "I don't think they understand. There are many ways to honor the dead, but for me and the anguished people who are my parishioners, I think the best way to honor them is not to die with them but to live. To try to live," he said.

Even though the cemetery problem is most acute in New York City, there are other cities where graveyards are being reclaimed for the use of the living. In June of 1967, the U.S. Department of Housing and Urban Development (HUD) approved a grant of $133,474 to the city of Pulaski, Tennessee, to convert a deteriorated public cemetery into a public park.

Announcing the approval of the grant, Charles M. Haar, then assistant secretary for metropolitan development said, "Through this demonstration, HUD's urban beautification program will for the first time seek ways to help cities restore abandoned and neglected public cemeteries to the role of community assets."

No one had been buried in the Old Pulaski Cemetery since 1888, and maintenance had gradually fallen off over the years. Finally it ceased. Weeds and unmowed grass covered the burial plots. Many of the markers had tilted out of position, others were crumbled, broken and lost under the growth of weeds.

Without disturbing the actual graves, headstones and monuments were cleaned, repaired and put in order. Landscaping followed. Walks were built and benches installed. Large, flat monuments had been set in a rubble stone wall built along one side of the park, and smaller gravestones were set on the top surfaces of several low curving walls so visitors could easily read the inscriptions. The free-standing monuments were redistributed throughout the park as sculptural elements and a new memorial structure was built as the central focus of the area.

What had long existed as an eyesore in Pulaski was transformed into a place of recreational value and historic interest. It now became a benefit instead of a detriment to the surrounding neighborhood.

The reclamation of the cemetery involved research into local questions of religious belief, custom, superstition, and legal regulation. It also required a campaign to achieve widespread public acceptance of the projected changes and consent from the heirs of those buried in the cemetery. The most valuable result of the Pulaski project was not the park itself, but the possible ramifications of the extensive report on cemetery reuse which has been published by HUD.

"In general," the HUD report concludes, "the citizens of Pulaski recognize the benefit of the rehabilitation. It is now a point of interest in Pulaski. No longer is the graveyard a blight or an eyesore. It is an asset in the city scape.

But of prime importance is the fact that the site now is permanently dedicated to open space."

While rehabilitation of old cemeteries is one way of providing both active and passive open-space areas, some advocate more aggressive measures such as graveyard relocation. In fact, large-scale relocations have already taken place. One of the most publicized of them occurred in San Francisco. In 1921 and 1923, because of land depletion for building sites, legislation was enacted to remove all cemeteries from the city and to prohibit further burials within city limits. Most cemeteries were moved to a small town, with a population of three hundred persons, south of San Francisco. The town of Colma soon became "Cemetery City," composed of some eleven hundred acres of crypts and tombstones. Colma has grown since then, and most of its citizens are in funeral-related businesses.

California law now allows relocation of cemeteries in any city with a population of a hundred thousand or greater.

Many still decry the relocation of cemeteries. In fact, however, graveyard relocation is nothing new or isolated. In Akron, Detroit, Houston, El Paso, and New Orleans existing cemeteries have been moved to make way for highways. In 1947, Baltimore relocated 170 graves to accommodate a new airport, and New York's traffic-snarled Brooklyn-Queens Expressway was built right through the center of Calvary Cemetery. In northeast Washington, D.C., the twenty-nine-acre Harmony Cemetery was relocated in its entirety to make way for a traffic interchange.

In 1967, Harold Ostroff, an official of the United Housing Fund, suggested to a New York City planning board that all cemeteries be removed from the city. The question was whether "to relocate the living or the dead," said Ostroff, who, noting cemeteries' tax-exempt status added, "Can we afford this $157 million tax exempt luxury for the dead when the problems of the living are so pressing?" Apparently New York can afford it, for the suggestion has not been pursued.

In the late 1960s Roger Starr, executive director of New York's Citizen's Housing and Planning Council, also suggested a massive relocation project whereby those interred within the city could be removed to another site.

The project would involve construction of a suitable memorial park, museum, and shrine. Starr suggested the place be Welfare Island in the East River. "In the description this sounds grotesque; in reality, with brilliant design and artful use of land, the island could provide a dignified and beautiful memorial. . . . Welfare Island is close enough to the population centers to stimulate repeated efforts to use its land constructively, but too far away to offer a useful site for housing or intensive recreation."

Starr suggested that the relocation be carried out over a period of many years. Even if it is not done, he notes, ultimately the city's cemeteries will be abandoned as the train of descendants relocate and become further removed. "Must we wait until it is upon us?" he asks.

At a density of fifty families per acre—modest by New York standards—it is estimated that the four thousand-plus acres presently occupied by New York City cemeteries could ultimately provide housing for two hundred thousand families. "Sensible use of the land could concentrate these families on two-thirds of the gross acreage, creating thirteen hundred acres of park, almost twenty-one Central Parks if one wished; or many smaller, connected parks." Such a project, Starr adds, would be a gain of "remarkable quality in the city's physical shape and structure, with consequent influence, one would hope, on its social problems. The cost is not so easily described: a sense that disturbing the dead is unseemly. But is that reaction sensitive or merely sentimental?"

To prevent the proliferation of further expanses of gray granite in urban areas, both groups and individuals have already embarked on new approaches to the function and design of the traditional cemetery. "The hodgepodge of monuments is depressing," says Martin Guadian of the National Association of Cemeteries. "In these days of ecological emphasis, we're looking to wide-open spaces. The object is to make cemeteries a beautiful place to visit."

Many new cemeteries do not permit conventional monuments. Graves are mainly designated with bronze, lawn-level markers which are small and allow for more graves per acre as well as easier upkeep of the grounds. Some of these parks, with their great, green rolling hills look more like golf courses than cemeteries.

In Seattle, Washington, in 1959, the Evergreen-Washelli Memorial Parks made an indefinite loan of five acres of as yet unused cemetery land to the Northwest Pony (baseball) League. At the time other space for organized ball games was nonexistent in the area. The league, of some two hundred boys, has built fields, bleachers, dugouts, concession stands, a parking area, backstops, and fences. They maintain the area themselves.

"Nobody's objected. The baseball field is separated from the burial area by undeveloped ground," says David Daley of Evergreen-Washelli. "Our theory is that we'd rather have the boys playing at the far end in an area set aside for them than in the regular part of the park."

The land at Evergreen-Washelli Memorial also has educational value. Because of the park's assortment of native and exotic plant species, art and botany classes from local schools are conducted there. "We have an open door policy. When you have 147 acres you have to. Anyone's welcome here unless he does something to the detriment of the park, and that doesn't happen very often," Daley adds.

Aside from these relatively few examples, imagination in the design of American cemeteries has been lacking. Roger Martin of the University of Minnesota's School of Architecture explains that "In the early evolution of landscape architecture in America the cemetery was a place to go and have picnics, to enrich one's life, rather than merely a place to inter one's dead. The present-day revival of the use of cemeteries other than for simple burial seems to me to be a very wise change, if for no other reason than the tremendous acreage involved."

Some countries have, for all practical purposes, already run out of burial space. In Japan and Italy bodies are stored for weeks at a time as burial space is sought. In Japan, officials encourage the use of "locker tombs" for permanent interment. There, land is in short supply anyway, even though 75 per cent of all persons who die are cremated. The locker tombs are contained in multistory concrete buildings with elevators and observation towers.

Future visitors to graveyards in Sao Paulo, Brazil, will also be able to ride in elevators—up thirty or more stories —to visit the tombs of the deceased. The architect credited with introducing the idea of vertical cemeteries in

Brazil is Fernando Martins Gomes, who explains, "Sao Paulo is a city where it is becoming increasingly difficult to die." His proposed hi-rise graveyards would contain morgue, autopsy facilities, funeral parlor, bar, and meeting rooms for visitors as well as a parking lot. "All this would prevent the trappings of death from becoming more lugubrious than death itself."

In busy Rio de Janeiro, where 4.5 million people are crowded into a tiny strip of land between mountains and the sea, the southern half of the city has already run out of cemetery space. Each burial in this area involves shifting of graves, and the cost of a burial plot has risen to about $5,000. People who live near the cemeteries have complained about ugly and pervasive odors, and in 1971 an Argentinian legislator seriously proposed that all corpses should be perfumed.

To solve Rio's problem, architect Dylardo Silva e Souza has planned a thirty-nine-story, $14.5 million cemetery. The skyscraper will contain, in addition to twenty-one thousand tombs with a capacity of one hundred and forty-seven thousand dead, a heliport, an eight-story garage, two churches, and twenty-one chapels.

George Plytas, mayor of Athens, Greece, announced in 1967 that his city had run out of burial space and had begun taking emergency measures to provide more graves for the dead. His short-term solution was to build a four-to-five-tier catacomb beneath a large existing cemetery near the Panathenian Stadium, site of the first modern Olympic Games in 1896.

Several United States undertakers have also been responsible for local innovations in burial and funeral practices. In Nashville, Tennessee, H. Raymond Ligon and his associates are building a twenty-story mausoleum that utilizes a "bedlike repose" for the viewing of the deceased. When completed his Woodlawn Cross Mausoleum and Funeral Home will house seventy-five thousand crypts. The finished building will occupy fourteen acres, but provide burial space equivalent to a one hundred-acre conventional cemetery. The Ligon method, which will be cheaper than a standard burial, is heralded by its promoters as the "first major change in twentieth century funeral equipment." The repose is available in "contemporary,

Early American, French Provincial, and Mediterranean" styles which "will individualize each funeral, yet eliminate the status symbols and high cost usually associated with caskets." Before being sent upstairs for permanent rest, the bodies will be enclosed by a sturdy, molded "Eternal-glass" covering which will lock into place forming an air-tight, watertight capsule.

In another typically American innovation, a twenty-year veteran of the undertaking business, Herschel Thornton of Atlanta, Georgia, has opened the nation's first drive-in mortuary. "Folks will be able just to drive by and view the last remains of their loved ones and then keep going." Thornton's moratorium has five plate glass windows from which the deceased are exhibited. "Help is so hard to get now. And there are the wages and hours laws. This way, folks can drive by at any time. It will be a great help for the elderly who can't get around too well. They can sit in their car and still pay their last respects," Thornton says.

A more traditional trend is the growing popularity of garden mausoleums, where caskets may be entombed five to six high in crypts. The J. C. Milne Company, of Portland, Oregon, has built more than two hundred of these containing more than one hundred thousand crypts over the past nineteen years. One such structure, being built for the Catholic diocese in Chicago, will eventually be the world's largest with some thirty thousand crypts.

Other space-saving practices are being carried out in United States cemeteries. One is the reduction of grave size from four by ten feet to three by eight feet. Another is family grave stacking or multiple burials, which are common in the nation's ninety-eight national cemeteries. Here widows are commonly buried in graves with their husbands.

Still another concept whose time may soon come is vertical ground burial. This is not an entirely new idea. A legend in southeastern Illinois speaks of an old flatboat pilot who died in the 1800s and requested burial "standing up" in a hillside cemetery above the Ohio River "so he could see the riverboats passing by." In London's Westminster Abbey, guides show visitors a small square memorial embedded in the floor among the other grave markers of Britain's most favorite sons.

It reads, "O Rare Ben Jonson," and the story behind it, they say, is that the poet once asked his monarch, Charles I, for a favor. "What is it?" demanded the king. "Give me eighteen square inches of ground," came the answer. "Where?" asked the king. "In Westminster Abbey." "Granted." And so Rare Ben was buried standing up under a pavement square of blue marble.

A 1967 study of cemeteries in the Hartford, Connecticut, area noted that vertical burials where the land is graded into stepped mounds or plateaus could be an effective saver of space and a pleasing element in the landscape. Nevertheless, vertical ground burial is yet to be accepted as commonplace.

An untold amount of burial space can be gained by the identification and resale of unused cemetery plots. Formerly it was the custom for families to buy a cemetery plot big enough for all of its members. But many of the plots went unused. This is even more common today in our highly mobile society. Many people simply never go home again, at least not to be buried. Says Roger Starr, "Someone should investigate the land tenure of families who haven't used their burial plots in years. After a certain period of time nobody even goes to visit. I wonder just how much land is irretrievably lost this way?"

Still another possibility—again rarely practiced in the United States because of cultural taboos—is the reuse of graves. In New York's Potters Field on Hart Island, some six hundred and fifty thousand bodies are buried on the site which has been in use since 1869. The grounds there are authorized for reuse every twenty-five years. But Potters Field is the burial place of the poor and the friendless. It is doubtful that one affluent American would be willing to share his final resting place with another—even after twenty-five years.

In Denmark many cemeteries are reused after fifteen years, and in 1970 West Berlin began to permit reuse of graves after fifty years. In 1932, Basel, Switzerland, pioneered another space-saving solution. The city council ruled that Basel's cemeteries occupied too much space and since then all burials have been on 125 acres of Hörnli Gottesaker, a hill on the outskirts of the city. The Basel municipal government pays for all burials and cremations and only the plainest of grave markers are allowed. The graves cost nothing and are maintained free—for a period of twenty years. After that, the family of the dead must buy the grave and pay a high price for maintenance, or the grave is reused. Most of them are reused.

Such grave recycling practices can be traced directly back to medieval times when churchyards were small and the parishioners of modest means. Next to the north wall of the chancel of many churches is a charnel house, or bone house. It was here that bones dug up from neighboring graves were tossed. In those days one could only hope to rest twenty or thirty years in a churchyard unless he was of a noble family that provided a fine tomb.

"Alas, poor Yorick, I knew him Horatio," lamented Prince Hamlet of Denmark when his court jester was dug up to make room for Ophelia's body.

Shakespeare was thoroughly familiar with such practices in his own country, as well as in the rest of Europe. Thus, even though the bard himself was a man of some consequences and a part-owner of the tithes of the church at Stratford-on-Avon, he felt the necessity to have this plea engraved upon his tombstone:

> Good Friend, for Jesu's sake forbear,
> To dig the dust inclosed here.
> Blest be the man that spares these stones,
> And curst be he that moves my bones.

Of course one of the most space-saving of all methods of body disposal is cremation. An urn of ashes, when buried, fills only a sixteen-inch square. Thus eight urns can be placed in the space taken up by one body buried in the currently traditional mode. Thousands of urns can be placed in a single, small memorial chapel.

In ancient times cremation was the general practice except in Egypt, China, and parts of Judea. In *Story of Primitive Man,* E. Clodd notes that cremation seemed to be "specially adapted by nomadic peoples, who, leaving their dead behind, would be unable to make provision for appeasing offerings at their graves. Hence the burning of the body to prevent the neglected ghost from following and harassing the living."

While cremation is now forbidden by Orthodox Jews, the Old Testament reveals that it was practiced by some Jews in ancient times. Saul, the first king of Israel, was cremated with his sons after battle with the Philistines at Mount Gilboa about 950 B.C. The book of Samuel says, "All the valiant men arose, and went all night and took the body of Saul and the bodies of his sons from the wall of Beth-shan, and came to Jabesh and burnt them there." Nowhere does the Bible forbid cremation or specify the mode of proper burial. Today's traditions and taboos have arisen in the intervening thousands of years and, it seems, new traditions could just as easily evolve again.

In 1963 the Roman Catholic Church altered its traditional prohibition of cremation and the practice is now accepted. Catholics long considered cremation a specific rejection of the prospect of resurrection and eternal life, but this argument was undermined when the Earl of Shaftsbury asked, "What will become of the blessed martyrs if the body cannot be returned to its original form by a wise and just God? The cremated remains of a saint are truly as venerable as his bones." Most Catholics and Orthodox Jews, however, still resist the idea of cremation; Protestants and liberal Jews account for most of the cremations in the United States.

Cremation was common practice among the early Greeks and Romans (and still is among Hindus). Amid the ruins atop Masada, one-time fortress of Herod the Great, archaeologists have discovered a circular building with niches scooped out of its interior walls. "It is our conviction," writes Israeli archaeologist, and chief of the Masada dig, Ygael Yadin, "that this building like similar though larger buildings discovered in Italy, was designed to receive the remains of cremations. It is probable that Herod built it for the burial of his servants, ministers or other members of his court who were not Jewish."

The first cremation reported in the United States was that of Colonel Henry Laurens, president of the Continental Congress in 1777 and 1778 and a member of George Washington's military staff. Laurens directed in his will that cremation was to take place and this was carried out in 1792 on his estate at Charleston, South Carolina.

It was not until 1876, however, that the first crematory was built in the United States, in Washington, Pennsylvania, by Dr. Francis Julius LeMoyne. It was built primarily for the cremation of his own body and the bodies of his friends. In 1913, Dr. Hugo Erichsen of Detroit organized the Cremation Association of America along the lines of a similar society in England. Today the association is essentially a trade organization made up of owners of crematories, columbariums, and memorial parks.

Since Dr. LeMoyne built his own crematory, the number of American cremations has increased along with the number of crematories. Between 1876 and 1884, 41 cremations were reported. In the next five years there were 731. From 1889 to 1894, there were nearly 3,000; and by 1899, the five-year total had reached 7,197. In 1900 alone, more than 6,000 were cremated. By that year there were 24 crematories operating in 15 states.

In 1970, some 250 crematories reported 88,150 cremations—up nearly 50 per cent from the 60,987 cremations in 1960.

The scientifically inclined explain that cremation is nothing more than a speeding up of nature's slow process of disposing of bodily remains. Cremation is merely burning or rapid oxidation as opposed to the oxidation process that would take place over many years in a standard burial.

In *The American Way of Death,* Jessica Mitford explains that "Cremation sounds like a simple, tidy solution to the disposal of the dead. . . . It is applauded by rationalists, people concerned with sanitation, land conservation and population statistics, and by those who would like to see an end to all the malarky that surrounds the usual kind of funeral."

However, even though cremation may entail less of a financial outlay, and a smaller involvement with casket buying and general funeral arrangements, it is not as simple as many would wish. In most cases the services of a funeral director are still required; embalming is still prescribed in most states, and, generally, a casket must be purchased and used, even though it is reduced to ashes along with the remains of the deceased.

Nevertheless, cremation is gaining in popularity in the United States—although at a slower pace than in many other nations around the world. An estimated 4.5 per cent of Americans who die today are cremated, but in Japan the figure is 75 per cent, and in England, where the rate is increasing, more than 50 per cent are cremated. In Sweden 25 per cent of the dead are cremated and in Denmark 29 per cent.

Harold Lamb, a Tacoma, Washington, cemetery owner, says, "It is my honest opinion that in twenty-five years cremation will be the law of the land. There is more cemetery property than park grounds in Tacoma right now and I know that isn't right and the younger people are going to realize that it isn't right too."

Others argue that the increase in cremation is a reaction to the more traditional "beautification of death." Cremation is fast, simple, and unassuming.

Some crematory managers say that as many as 50 per cent of families request no funeral at all and many others choose more personal and less religious services.

In the United States the practice of cremation varies considerably with the geography. The four Pacific Coast States of California, Oregon, Washington, and Nevada accounted for about 37,500 of the cremations in 1970, while in Minnesota, Nebraska, Iowa, Missouri, Texas, Oklahoma, and Kansas there were only about 3,500. In Tacoma, Washington, 17 per cent of the dead were cremated, but in Pittsburgh the figure was only 2.5 per cent.

Some have suggested that the demand for cremation is greater on the West Coast because so many of its residents have relocated from other parts of the country—far away from family cemetery plots and the home towns of their birth. Furthermore, the West Coast has always been a pioneer in breaking with social tradition. According to Herbert Hargrave, secretary of the Cremation Association of America, "So many people have come to the Pacific Coast from Eastern areas and have cut off their original home ties. They seem to be willing to adopt the custom prevalent here."

Reports also indicate that increasing numbers of persons are spurning the funeral-industry encouraged tradition of keeping cremated remains in a costly urn in perpetual gardens or columbaria. The scattering of ashes at sea or over the land is no longer a rarity. Each day along the coast of Southern California, there are between twenty-five and thirty-five burials of ashes at sea, about half of them being scattered from airplanes. The numbers of such burials are expected to increase rapidly because of a new state law that outlaws the widespread practice of requiring the purchase of a coffin for all cremations.

One California widow, who decided to have her husband's remains cremated said, "It just seemed a lot purer. I didn't need all of that ritual and all of that sobbing around the graveside. In retrospect the fact that the body was destroyed also makes it easier for me to accept the finality of death. It's better than thinking of some little spot where he's buried."

SELECTED BIBLIOGRAPHY

CHAPTER 1. REVISING THE CRITERIA OF DEATH

Ackerknecht, Erwin. "Death in the History of Medicine." *Bulletin of the History of Medicine,* January–February 1968.

Ad Hoc Committee of the Harvard Medical School to Examine the Definition of Brain Death. "A Definition of Irreversible Coma." *Journal of the American Medical Association,* August 5, 1968.

Ayd, Frank J., Jr. "What Is Death?" Paper presented at the Second National Congress on Medical Ethics, Judicial Council of the American Medical Association, Chicago, October 5, 6, 1968.

———. Personal communication.

"Back from the Dead." *Newsweek,* November 13, 1967.

Biörck, Gunnar. "On the Definitions of Death," *World Medical Journal,* November 1967.

Black, H. C., *Black's Law Dictionary.* St. Paul: West Publishing Co., 1951.

Cohn, Victor. "Our Old Concepts of Death Seen Changing." *Washington Post*, May 29, 1972.

"Death, When Is Thy Sting?" *Newsweek*, August 19, 1968.

"Defining Death." *Science News Magazine*, August 24, 1968.

Dowd, Donald W., ed. *Medical Moral and Legal Implications of Recent Medical Advances*. New York: DeCapo Press, 1971.

Durdin, Tillman. "Physicians Adopt a Code on Death." *New York Times*, August 10, 1968.

Fermaglich, Joseph. "Determining Cerebral Death." *Annals of Family Practice*, March 1971.

Gray et al. v. Sawyer et al. (247 S.W. 2d 496).

Hamlin, Hannibal. "Life or Death by EEG." *Journal of the American Medical Association*, October 12, 1964.

Herold, Justin. "Signs and Tests of Death." *New Orleans Medical and Surgical Journal*, 1899.

Kennedy, Ian M. "The Kansas Statute on Death—An Appraisal." *New England Journal of Medicine*, October 21, 1971.

Korein, Julius. Personal communication.

————, and Maccario, Micheline. "On the Diagnosis of Cerebral Death: A Prospective Study on 55 Patients to Define Irreversible Coma." Unpublished, 1970.

Lamb, Lawrence. Personal communication.

Mohandas, A., and Chou, S. N. "Criteria of Brain Death." *Journal of Neurology*, August 1971.

Muller, Pierre H. "Legal Medicine and the Delimitation of Death." *World Medical Journal*, November 1967.

Poe, William D. *The Old Person in Your Home*. New York: Scribner's, 1969.

Pope Pius XII. "The Prolongation of Life." Address to the International Congress of Anesthesiologists, November 4, 1958.

Rosenfeld, Albert. *The Second Genesis*. Englewood Cliffs, N.J.: Prentice-Hall, 1969.

Silverman, Daniel; Saunders, Michael; Schwab, Robert; and Masland, Richard. "Cerebral Death and the Electroencephalogram," *Journal of the American Medical Association*, September 8, 1969.

Smith v. Smith. (317 S.W. 2d 275).

Snider, Arthur. "A Score Card for Death." *Science Digest*, August 1970.

Stengel, Walter. Personal communication.

Task Force on Death and Dying, Institute of Society, Ethics

and the Life Sciences. "Refinements in Criteria for the Determination of Death: An Appraisal." *Journal of the American Medical Association,* July 3, 1972.

Taylor, Loren F. "A Statutory Definition of Death in Kansas." *Journal of the American Medical Association,* January 11, 1971.

"Texas Heart Transplant Raises Legal Questions." *New York Times,* May 13, 1968.

Thomson, Elizabeth. "The Role of Physicians in the Humane Societies of the Eighteenth Century." *Bulletin of the History of Medicine,* January–February 1963.

Toynbee, Arnold and others, *Man's Concern with Death.* New York: McGraw-Hill, 1968.

"What is Life? When is Death?" *Time,* May 27, 1966.

Williamson, P. William. "Life or Death—Whose Decision." *Journal of the American Medical Association,* September 5, 1966.

Winter, Arthur, ed. *The Moment of Death: A Symposium.* Springfield, Ill.: Charles C. Thomas, 1969.

Woodruff, M. F. A. "The Ethics of Organ Transplantation." *British Medical Journal,* June 6, 1964.

Wright, Irving S. "Who Should Make the Decisions." In *The Moment of Death.* Edited by A. Winter. Springfield, Ill.: Charles C. Thomas, 1969.

CHAPTER 2. TRANSPLANTS: *You Can Take It with You*

Bar-Ilan University. "Professor Takes Israeli Rabbis and Pathologists to Task in Current Autopsy Controversy." Undated communication to the press, received early 1972.

Bishop, Jerry. "Medical Experts Urge Wider Use of Autopsies to Confirm Diagnosis." *Wall Street Journal,* November 22, 1971.

"The Cadaver Boom," *Newsweek,* April 17, 1972.

Carr, Jesse, and Leydet, François. "What Organ Transplants Mean to Your Life," *Vogue,* October 15, 1968.

Cleary, David M. "I'm Giving My Body to Science." *Philadelphia Evening Bulletin,* October 16, 1970.

Diamond, Edwin. "Are We Ready to Leave Our Bodies to the Next Generation?" *New York Times Magazine,* April 21, 1968.

Dukeminier, J., Jr., and Sanders, D. "Organ Transplantation: A Proposal for Routing Salvaging of Cadaver Organs." *New England Journal of Medicine,* August 1968.

Fisher, Russell. "Let the Dead Help the Living." *Today's Health,* April 1969.

"Harvesting the Body." *Newsweek,* March 3, 1969.

Head, Robert. Personal communication.

Hendin, David. "The Morality of Transplants." *Columbia Missourian,* July 6, 1969.

———. "Medical Center Restores Penitentiary Inmate's Sight." *Columbia Missourian,* June 27, 1969.

Karpel, Craig. "Immortality Is Fully Deductible." *Playboy,* September 1971.

Ladimer, Irving. *The Challenge of Transplantation.* New York: Public Affairs Committee, 1970.

———. "Transplantation." New York State Department of Health. *Health News,* April 1971.

Lynch, John J. "Ethics of the Heart Transplant." *America,* February 10, 1968.

Marley, Faye. "Let the Dead Help the Living." *Science News,* January 28, 1967.

Middleton, John. "Bold New Views on Getting Organs for Transplants." *Medical Economics,* June 7, 1971.

Mitford, Jessica. *The American Way of Death.* New York: Simon and Schuster, 1963.

Murray, Joseph, and Barnes, B. A. "Organ Transplant Registry." *Journal of the American Medical Association,* September 13, 1971.

"Repairs, Implants, Transplants . . . A New Era for Medicine." *U.S. News and World Report,* January 22, 1968.

Sadler, Alfred, Jr., and Sadler, B. L. "Recent Developments in the Legal Aspects of Transplantation in the United States." *Transplantation Proceedings,* March 1971.

Sadler, Alfred, Jr.; Sadler, Blair; and Schreiner, George. "A Uniform Card for Organ and Tissue Donation." *Modern Medicine,* December 29, 1969.

Schreiner, George. Personal communication.

Uniform Anatomical Gifts Act. Drafted by the National Conference of Commissioners on Uniform State Laws, July 30, 1968.

United States Department of Health, Education and Welfare. "Research Advances in Human Transplantation." Bethesda, Md.: General Clinical Research Centers Branch, National Institutes of Health, 1970.

Veith, Ilza. "Historical Reflections on Organ Transplants." *Modern Medicine,* March 25, 1968.

CHAPTER 3. EUTHANASIA: *Let There Be Death*

"Adult Jehovah's Witness and Blood Transfusions." *Journal of the American Medical Association,* January 10, 1972.

Anonymous. "A New Way of Dying." *Atlantic Monthly,* January 1957.

Ayd, Frank J., Jr. "Voluntary Euthanasia: The Right To Be Killed." *Medical Counterpoint,* June 1970.

Barnard, Christiaan, and Pepper, C. B. *One Life,* New York: Macmillan, 1970.

Collins, Vincent. "Should We Let Them Die?" *Saturday Evening Post,* May 1962.

"Courts Differ on Patients' Rights in Refusing Care." *American Medical News,* September 6, 1971.

"Death With Dignity: A Recommendation for Statutory Change." *University of Florida Law Review* 22 (1970).

"Dies after Court Stays Scalpel." *New York Daily News* (UPI), July 5, 1971.

"Dilemma in Dying." *Time,* July 19, 1971.

"Dying Woman Wins Court Plea to Stop Terminal Surgery." *New York Times* (UPI), July 3, 1971.

"Euthanasia at 80?" *Newsweek,* May 12, 1969.

Euthanasia Educational Fund. *The Right to Die with Dignity.* Proceedings of First Euthanasia Conference, November 23, 1968.

————. *Today's Student Takes a New Look at Life and Death.* Proceedings of Second Euthanasia Conference, December 6, 1969.

————. *Attitudes toward Euthanasia in Ancient Times and Today.* Proceedings of Third Euthanasia Conference, December 5, 1970.

"Euthanasia in England: A Growing Storm." *America,* May 2, 1970.

Ferriar, J. "On Treatment of Dying." *Medical Histories and Reflections,* London 1798.

Fletcher, Joseph. "The Patient's Right to Die." *Harpers Magazine,* October 1960.

————. "Anti-Dysthanasia: The Problem of Prolonging Death." Paper presented at the annual meeting of the Euthanasia Society, February 26, 1962.

————. "Voluntary Euthanasia: The New Shape of Death." *Medical Counterpoint,* June 1970.

"Heroic Treatment." *Medical Tribune,* April 10, 1961.

Hinton, John. *Dying,* Baltimore, Md.: Penguin Books, 1967.

"Is There No Right to Die?" *Bergen Record* (Hackensack, N.J.), July 20, 1971.

Jakobovits, Immanuel. *Jewish Medical Ethics,* New York: Philosophical Library, 1959.

————. "The Dying and Their Treatment in Jewish Law." *Hebrew Medical Journal* 2 (1961):251.

Kass, Leon. "Death as an Event." *Science,* August 20, 1971.

Lasagna, Louis. *Life, Death and the Doctor.* New York: Knopf, 1968.

"Let the Hopelessly Ill Die?" *U.S. News and World Report,* July 1, 1968.

McIntyre, Ray V. "Voluntary Euthanasia: The Ultimate Perversion." *Medical Counterpoint,* June 1970.

Milwaukee Journal, January 21–25, 1972. Articles on the Gertrude Raasch case.

Milwaukee Sentinel, January 22–February 1, 1972. Articles on the Gertrude Raasch case.

Morrison, Robert S. "Death, Process or Event?" *Science,* August 20, 1971.

"There is No 'Constitutional Right' to Die." Schering Corporation. *Physician's Legal Brief,* November 1971.

Pope Pius XII. "Morality of Pain Prevention." *Catholic Mind,* May–June 1957.

"The Right to Die." *America,* August 3, 1968.

" 'Right to Die' Court Decision May Aid Proponents of Euthanasia Law." *The Nation's Health,* August 1971.

Rosner, Fred. "Jewish Attitude toward Euthanasia." *Medical Judaica,* January–March, 1972.

Sackett, Walter, Jr. "Death With Dignity." *Medical Opinion and Review,* June 1969.

————. "An Act Relating to the Right to Die with Dignity." HB 2614, State of Florida, 1971.

Sullivan, Michael T. Personal communication.

Waggoner, W. H. "Court Overrules Wife on Surgery." *New York Times,* January 28, 1972.

Williams, Glanville. *The Sanctity of Life and the Criminal Law,* New York: Knopf, 1966.

Williams, R. H. "Our Role in the Generation, Modification, and Termination of Life." *Archives of Internal Medicine,* August 1969.

Wolfe, R. I. Letter to the editor. *Science,* February 11, 1972.

"Abe Maslow—1908–1970," editorial. *Psychology Today*, August 1970.

Brim, Orville; Freeman, Howard; Levine, Sol; and Scotch, Norman, eds. *The Dying Patient*, New York: Russell Sage Foundation, 1970.

"Christmas at St. Christopher's." *American Journal of Nursing*, December 16, 1971.

Danto, Bruce L. "Suicide and Psychopharmacologic Agents in the Cancer Patient." Paper presented at seminar of the Thanatology Foundation, Columbia College of Physicians and Surgeons, November 12, 1971.

Feifel, Herman. "Attitudes toward Death in Some Normal and Mentally Ill Populations." In *The Meaning of Death*. Edited by H. Feifel. New York: McGraw-Hill, 1959.

————. "Death." In *Taboo Topics*. Edited by N. L. Faberow. New York: Atherton Press, 1963.

Grof, Stanislav; Pahnke, Walter; Goodman, Louis and Kurland, Albert. "Psychedelic Drug Assisted Psychotherapy in Patients with Terminal Cancer." Paper presented at seminar of the Thanatology Foundation, Columbia College of Physicians and Surgeons, November 12, 1971.

Hinton, John. *Dying*. Baltimore, Md.: Penguin Books, 1967.

Krant, Melvin. "The Organized Care of the Dying Patient." *Hospital Practice*, January 1972.

Kübler-Ross, Elisabeth K. *On Death and Dying*. New York: Macmillan, 1969.

————. "Psychology of Dying." Paper presented to the American Academy of Family Practice, Miami Beach, November 5, 1971.

————. "On the Use of Psychopharmacologic Agents for the Dying Patient and the Bereaved." Paper presented at seminar of the Thanatology Foundation, Columbia College of Physicians and Surgeons, November 12, 1971.

Kutscher, Austin. Speech to seminar of the Thanatology Foundation, Columbia College of Physicians and Surgeons, November 12, 1971.

Mark, Lester C., and Kutscher, Austin H. "Acupuncture: A Statement Concerning Terminal Care and Anticipatory Grief." Paper presented at seminar on Psychological Aspects of Anticipatory Grief, Columbia University College of Physicians and Surgeons, April 14, 1972.

Middleton, Warren C. "Some Reactions toward Death among College Students." *Journal of Abnormal and Social Psychology* 31 (1936).

Noyes, Russell, Jr. "The Act of Death: The Art of Treatment." *Medical Insight,* March 1971.

———. "The Art of Dying." *Perspectives in Biology and Medicine,* Spring 1971.

———. "The Care and Management of the Dying." *Archives of Internal Medicine,* August 1971.

Osler, Sir William. *Science and Immortality in the Student Life and Other Essays.* Boston: Houghton Mifflin, 1931.

Phillips, David P. "Birthdays and Death." Paper presented to the American Sociological Association, San Francisco, September 1969.

———. "Deaths before and after the Birthday." Unpublished manuscript dated September 1970.

Powers, Thomas. "Learning to Die." *Harpers Magazine,* June 1971.

Ramsey, Paul. *The Patient as Person: Explorations in Medical Ethics.* New Haven: Yale University Press, 1970.

Rollins, Hyder S., ed. *The Keats Circle.* Cambridge, Mass.: Harvard University Press, 1965.

Rosenbaum, Connie. Four-part series on death, *St. Louis Post-Dispatch,* September 13–16, 1971.

Saunders, Cicely. "The Treatment of Intractable Pain in Terminal Cancer." *Proceedings of the Royal Society of Medicine,* March 1963.

———. "The Last Stages of Life." *American Journal of Nursing,* March 1965.

———. "Telling Patients." *District Nursing,* September 1965.

———. "Watch with Me." *Nursing Times,* November 26, 1965.

———. *The Management of Terminal Illness.* London: Hospital Medicine Publications Ltd., 1967.

Toynbee, Arnold and others, *Man's Concern with Death.* New York: McGraw-Hill, 1968.

Twycross, R. G. Paper presented at seminar of the Thanatology Foundation, Columbia College of Physicians and Surgeons, November 12, 1971.

Wald, Florence. Personal communication.

Weisman, A. D., and Hackett, J. P. "Predilection to Death." *Psychosomatic Medicine* 23 (1961).

Woodward, Kenneth. "How America Lives with Death." *Newsweek,* April 6, 1970.

"Dealing With Death." *Medical World News,* May 21, 1971.

"Do You Often Lose Touch with a Dying Patient?" *Patient Care Magazine,* May 31, 1970.

Easson, W. M. "Care of the Young Patient Who Is Dying." *Journal of the American Medical Association,* July 22, 1968.

Feifel, Herman, "Physicians Consider Death." Paper presented at seventy-fifth annual convention, American Psychological Association, September 1967.

Glaser, Barney G., and Strauss, Anselm L. *Awareness of Dying.* Chicago: Aldine, 1965.

————. "Awareness of Dying." In *Loss and Grief.* New York: Columbia University Press, 1970.

————. "Patterns of Dying." In *The Dying Patient.* New York: Russell Sage Foundation, 1970.

Gorer, Geoffrey. *Death, Grief and Mourning.* New York: Doubleday, 1965.

Greene, William A. "The Physician and His Dying Patient." Paper presented at the conference, "The Patient, Death, and the Family," University of Rochester School of Medicine, April 29, 1971.

Hinton, John. "The Physical and Mental Distress of the Dying." *Quarterly Journal of Medicine,* January 1963.

————. *Dying.* Baltimore, Md.: Penguin Books, 1967.

Lasagna, Louis. *Life, Death and the Doctor.* New York: Knopf, 1968.

————. "Physicians' Behavior toward the Dying Patient." In *The Dying Patient.* New York: Russell Sage Foundation, 1970.

Osler, Sir William. *Aequanimitas.* 3d ed. New York: McGraw-Hill, 1932.

Pemberton, L. Beaty. "Most Terminal Patients Should Be Told." *Chronic Disease Management,* October 1971.

Peretz, David. "Development, Object-Relationships, and Loss." In *Loss and Grief.* New York: Columbia University Press, 1970.

"Physicians Do Inform Terminal Patients." *Chronic Disease Management,* October 1971.

Poe, William. "Marantology: A Needed Specialty." *New England Journal of Medicine,* January 13, 1972.

————. Personal communication.

Rabin, D. L., and Rabin, L. H. "Consequences of Death for Physicians, Nurses and Hospitals." In *The Dying Patient.* New York: Russell Sage Foundation, 1970.

Schoenberg, Bernard. "Management of the Dying Patient." In *Loss and Grief.* New York: Columbia University Press, 1970.

Thompson, Thomas. *Hearts.* New York: McCall Books, 1972.

Wahl, C. W. "The Fear of Death." *Bulletin of the Menninger Clinic* 22 (1958).

"What Are Your Attitudes toward the Dying Process?" *Patient Care Magazine*, May 31, 1970.

Wiener, Jerry M. "Response of Medical Personnel to the Fatal Illness of a Child." In *Loss and Grief*, New York: Columbia University Press, 1970.

CHAPTER 6. CHILDREN AND DEATH

Char, Walter F. "Death, Dying as Viewed by a Psychiatrist." *Honolulu Star-Bulletin*, May 12–22, 1970. Reprint of nine-article series on death.

"Focus on the Patient Not on the Fact of His Dying." *Patient Care Magazine*, May 31, 1970.

Friedman, Stanford B. "Communication within the Family of a Fatally Ill Child." Paper presented at the conference, "The Patient, Death, and the Family." University of Rochester School of Medicine, April 30, 1971.

Furman, Robert A. "The Child's Reaction to Death in the Family." In *Loss and Grief.* New York: Columbia University Press, 1970.

Gardner, D. Bruce. *Development in Early Childhood: The Pre-school Years.* New York: Harper and Row, 1964.

Gardner, George. *The Emerging Personality.* New York: Delacorte, 1970.

Ginott, Haim. *Between Parent and Child.* New York: Macmillan, 1965.

"Help for the Family before and after a death." *Patient Care Magazine*, May 31, 1970.

"How Well Prepared Are You for Death in the Young." *Patient Care Magazine*, May 31, 1970.

Ilg, Francis L., and Ames, Louise. *The Gesell Institute's Book of Child Behavior.* New York: Harper and Row, 1955.

Kübler-Ross, Elisabeth. "Death and the Child." Lecture at the workshop, "Caring for the Dying Child and His Family," Babies Hospital, Columbia Presbyterian Medical Center, January 21, 1972.

Morrison, Robert. Preface to *The Dying Patient*. New York: Russell Sage Foundation, 1970.

Olshaker, Bennett. *What Shall We Tell The Kids?* New York: Arbor House, 1971.

————. Personal communication.

Rosenbaum, Connie. Four-part series on death. *St. Louis Post-Dispatch,* September 13–16, 1971.

Schowalter, John E. "The Child's Reaction to His Own Terminal Illness." In *Loss and Grief.* New York: Columbia University Press, 1970.

Spock, Benjamin. *Baby and Child Care.* New York: Pocket Books, 1968.

Watt, Anne S. "Helping Children to Mourn I." *Medical Insight,* July 1971.

————. "Helping Children to Mourn II." *Medical Insight,* August 1971.

Yudkin, Simon. "Death and the Young." In *Man's Concern with Death.* Edited by Arnold Toynbee and others. New York: McGraw-Hill, 1968.

CHAPTER 7. GRIEF AND BEREAVEMENT

Anderson, Robert. "Notes of a Survivor." Paper presented at the conference, "The Patient, Death, and the Family," University of Rochester School of Medicine, April 29, 1971.

Battin, Delia. Personal communication.

"The Bereaved as Patients." Hoffmann LaRoche. *Image,* October 1971.

Birbaum, Philip. *A Book of Jewish Concepts.* New York: Hebrew Publishing, 1964.

"Broken Heart Syndrome." *Newsweek,* October 23, 1967.

Cohen, Harry A. *A Basic Jewish Encyclopedia.* Hartford, Conn.: Hartmore House, 1965.

Freud, Sigmund. "Mourning and Melancholia." In *Collected Papers of Sigmund Freud,* vol. 4. London: Hogarth Press, 1956.

Fulton, Robert L., and Geis, Gilbert. "Social Change and Social Conflict: The Rabbi and the Funeral Director." Western Kentucky University Sociological Symposium, Fall 1968.

"Good Grief." *Scientific American*, April 1969.

Gorer, Geoffrey. *Death, Grief and Mourning.* New York: Doubleday, 1965.

Hinton, John. *Dying.* Baltimore, Md.: Penguin Books, 1967.

Kane, John J. "The Irish Wake: A Sociological Appraisal." Western Kentucky University Sociological Symposium, Fall 1968.

Kutscher, Austin, ed. *But Not to Lose.* New York: Frederick Fell, 1969.

————. "Practical Aspects of Bereavement." Paper presented at seminar of the Thanatology Foundation, Columbia College of Physicians and Surgeons, November 12, 1971.

Lindemann, E. "Symptomatology and Management of Acute Grief." *American Journal of Psychiatry* 101 (1944): 141.

Lorenz, Konrad. *On Aggression.* New York: Harcourt, 1966.

Maddison, David, and Raphael, Beverly. "Normal Bereavement as an Illness Requiring Care." Paper presented at seminar of the Thanatology Foundation, Columbia College of Physicians and Surgeons, November 12, 1971.

Parkes, C. Murray. "Effects of Bereavement on Physical and Mental Health: A Study of the Medical Records of Widows." *British Medical Journal* 2 (1964):274.

————. "The First Year of Bereavement: A Longitudinal Study of the Reactions of London Widows to the Death of Their Husband." *Psychiatry*, November 1970.

Peretz, David. "Reaction to Loss." In *Loss and Grief.* New York: Columbia University Press, 1970.

————. "Development, Object-Relationship and Loss." In *Loss and Grief.* New York: Columbia University Press, 1970.

Rees, W. Dewi. Two untitled papers on grief presented at seminar of the Thanatology Foundation, Columbia College of Physicians and Surgeons, November 12, 1971.

————. and Lutkins, Sylvia G. "Mortality of Bereavement." *British Medical Journal*, October 1967.

Salomone, Jerome J. "An Empirical Report on Some Controversial American Funeral Practices." Western Kentucky University Sociological Symposium, Fall 1968.

Schmale, A. H. "Coping Reactions of the Cancer Patient and His Family." *Catastrophic Illness in the Seventies.* New York: Cancer Care, Inc. 1971.

————. "Normal Grief Is Not a Disease." Paper presented at seminar of the Thanatology Foundation, Columbia College of Physicians and Surgeons, November 12, 1971.

Silverman, Phyllis R. "Factors Involved in Accepting an Offer of Help." *Archives of the Foundation of Thanatology,* Fall 1971.

————. "The Widow-to-Widow Program: An Experiment in Preventive Intervention." *Mental Hygiene,* July 1969.

Stitt, Abby. "Emergency after Death." *Emergency Medicine,* March 1971.

Weiner, Alfred. Personal communication.

————. "The Use of Psychopharmacologic Agents in the Management of the Bereaved." Paper presented at seminar of the Thanatology Foundation, Columbia College of Physicians and Surgeons, November 12, 1971.

CHAPTER 8. DEATH AND THE DEEP FREEZE

Comfort, Alex. "Imitations of Immortality." *Medical Opinion,* June 1971.

"Cryobiology." *Time,* February 3, 1967.

Cryonics Reports, November 1966; February 1969.

Ettinger, Robert C. W. *The Prospect of Immortality.* New York: Doubleday, 1964.

————. "The Frozen Christian." *Christian Century,* October 27, 1965.

————. "Cryonics and the Purpose of Life." *Christian Century,* October 4, 1967.

Habenstein, Robert W., and Lamers, William. *The History of American Funeral Directing.* Milwaukee: Bulfin Printers, Inc., 1955.

Hare, Burt. "Mummies: Man's Drive for Immortality." *Science Digest,* December 1969.

Harrington, Alan. *The Immortalist.* New York: Random House, 1969.

Horn, Frederick. Personal communication.

Immortality, June–July 1970; August–September 1970; Winter 1971; Spring 1971.

"An Interview with a Prospective Suspension Patient." *Cryonics Review,* April 1969.

Konikova, A. S.; Pogasova, A.; and Nikulin, V. "Restoration of Protein Synthesis after Death and the Effect of Postmortal Cooling." *Nature New Biology,* January 19, 1972.

Konner, Joan. "What Man Shall Live and Not See Death." WNBC Television, New York, September 8, 1971.

Neugebauer, William. "Mother Sees Hope in Freezing Son's Body." *New York Daily News,* August 2, 1968.

Sherman, J. K. "Immortality and the Freezing of Human Bodies." *Natural History,* December 1971.

Warshofsky, Fred. *The Rebuilt Man.* New York: Thomas Crowell, 1965.

Wilford, John N. "Body of Student at NYU is Frozen." *New York Times,* August 2, 1968.

CHAPTER 9. MAKE WAY FOR THE LIVING

"Athens Short of Graves, Plans to Build Catacomb." *New York Times* (AP), March 12, 1967.

Chard, Chester S. *Man in Prehistory.* New York: McGraw-Hill, 1969.

Cremation Association of America. "Why Cremation?" 1967.
———. "Statistical Report for Years 1960–1970."

Darntown, John. "Pinelawn Is a Prosperous City of the Dead." *New York Times,* February 21, 1971.

Davis, W. S. *Life in Elizabethan Days.* New York: Harper and Row, 1930.

"Dilemma of a Cemetery-Park." *New York Times,* August 23, 1967.

Fosburgh, Lacy. "St. Mark's Building Playground in Its Cemetery, the City's Oldest." *New York Times,* February 9, 1970.

Fraser, C. G. "City Witness Calls for Housing in Central Park and Cemeteries." *New York Times,* September 26, 1967.

Habenstein, Robert W. and Lamers, William. *The History of American Funeral Directing.* Milwaukee: Bulfin Printers, Inc., 1965.

Hargrave, Herbert R. Personal communication.

"High Cost of Dying Spurs an Increase in Cremation and Burial among Southern Californians." *New York Times,* November 14, 1971.

Ligon, H. Raymond. Personal communication.

Mitford, Jessica. *The American Way of Death.* New York: Simon and Schuster, 1963.

Puckle, B. S. *Funeral Customs.* London: T. Werner Laurie Ltd., 1926.

Polson, C. J.; Brittain, R. P.; and Marshall, T. K. *The Disposal of the Dead.* Springfield, Ill.: Charles C. Thomas, 1962.

"Raising the Dead." *Time,* November 29, 1971.

Shipler, David K. "Proposal for Park in Cemetery Assailed as 'Ghoulish.' " *New York Times,* August 6, 1969.

"Space for the Living." *Open Space Action,* September–October 1969.

Starr, Roger. "An Immodest Proposal." Manuscript of an article prepared for the *Village Voice,* May 1969.

"Undertaker Will offer New Drive-In Service" (UPI) March 14, 1968.

United States Columbarium Co., Inc. "The Story of Cremation." 1970.

United States Department of Housing and Urban Development. *Cemeteries as Open Space Reservations.* Washington, D.C.: Government Printing Office, 1970.

————. *Commemorative Parks from Abandoned Public Cemeteries: A Legal Report.* Washington, D.C.: Government Printing Office, 1971.

Vidal, David J. "High Rise Graves On Way?" *New York Post* (AP), August 30, 1971.

Yadin, Yigael. *Masada,* New York: Random House, 1966.

INDEX

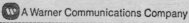